To Pat —
August 15, 1979
Love always,
Barbara

D0934578

COURAGE
FOR
CRISIS LIVING

COURAGE
FOR
CRISIS LIVING

Paul L. Walker, Ph.D.

Fleming H. Revell Company
Old Tappan, New Jersey

Library of Congress Cataloging in Publication Data

Walker, Paul L.
    Courage for crisis living.

    1.   Christian life—Church of God authors.   I.   Title.
BV4501.2.W32   248'.48'673   78-5099
ISBN 0-8007-0931-4

TO my sons: Paul and Mark
Two young men of whom
I am very proud

Contents

Foreword   9
Preface   11

1 Courage for Crisis Living   13
   Crisis Point—Environmental Pressures
   Scriptural Resource—Joshua 1:1–9
   Courage Builders—Stake your claim; sort out
   your faith; stay in touch
2 The Paradox of Being OK   22
   Crisis Point—Personal Adjustment
   Scriptural Resource—Philippians 3:13, 14
   Courage Builders—Forget the past; face up to
   the future; press for the present
3 Will the Real You Please Stand Up!   30
   Crisis Point—Identity Distortion
   Scriptural Resources—Psalms 8:4, 5; Psalms
   139:14; Ephesians 4:24
   Courage Builders—You are incomparable; you
   are invisible; you are invincible
4 From Fractured Feelings to a Functional Faith   42
   Crisis Point—Guilt Reactions
   Scriptural Resource—John 21:1–18
   Courage Builders—Accent your faith; accept
   your opportunities; actualize your calling
5 You Can Win With Worry   52
   Crisis Point—Worrisome Stress
   Scriptural Resource—Philippians 4:6–8
   Courage Builders—Pray in detail; practice the
   peace of God; program your thinking
6 You Can Defuse Depression   61
   Crisis Point—Depression Experiences

Scriptural Resource—1 Kings 19:7–18

Courage Builders—Recognize that life moves in cycles; function, whether you feel like it or not; touch your assurance point; get outside of yourself

7   From Handicaps to Handles   71

     Crisis Point—Adverse Limitations

     Scriptural Resource—2 Corinthians 4:16, 17

     Courage Builders—Research your resources; re-tune your responses; reorder your priorities

8   Which Way Is Up?   79

     Crisis Point—Confused Circumstances

     Scriptural Resources—Matthew 9:1–6; Matthew 14:22–33; John 16:33

     Courage Builders—Experience a miracle of forgiveness; expect a miracle of faithfulness; express a miracle of forcefulness

9   You Can Live on Top When the Bottom Drops Out   90

     Crisis Point—Distress Situations

     Scriptural Resources—Job 1:1–5, 22; Job 6:8–13; Job 13:15, 16; Job 42:10

     Courage Builders—Acknowledge distress as a fact; activate determination as a force; anticipate deliverance as a fulfillment

10   An Inside Look at the Outside Life   102

     Crisis Point—Inefficient life-style

     Scriptural Resource—Colossians 1:9–11

     Courage Builders—Develop a productive purpose; internalize a productive process; exercise a productive power

11   Positive Power in Negative Times   116

     Crisis Point—Negative Adjustment Patterns

     Scriptural Resource—Romans 8:1, 14–17

     Courage Builders—Change your walk; follow the Spirit; renounce fear; claim your heritage

Foreword

Every few years a Christian book comes along in which a topic of critical importance is matched with an author who is perfectly equipped to write about it. When that rare combination occurs, the result is always a book of extraordinary impact.

This is such a book and just such an ideal match of a man and his subject. When Dr. Paul L. Walker writes about life's crises and the sources of courage from which a Christian can draw, he knows what he is talking about. When he integrates the principles of psychology and evangelical theology, neither perspective is slighted. Doctor Walker's academic background is equally impressive in theology (an honors Masters of Divinity graduate of Emory University's Candler School of Theology) and in counseling (a Ph.D. in Counseling Psychology from Georgia State University).

The insights he shares in this book come not so much from the classroom, however, as from life itself. For seventeen years he has pastored the Mount Paran Church of God in Atlanta, a congregation of three thousand worshipers, many of whom drive long distances each week to draw "courage for crisis living" from his preaching and counseling. During his pastorate, his congregation has more than quadrupled in size, and overflow crowds pack the Mount Paran sanctuary every Sunday.

I served as an assistant to Dr. Walker for four years and, during that period, heard him preach over three hundred times. He is widely known in Atlanta as a brilliant preacher, and I don't believe that among those three hundred sermons I ever heard a poor one. But it is in the quieter, more private encounters that he is perhaps at his best. As a counselor, he has helped hundreds of people find answers to their own tough problems.

In either role, Dr. Paul Walker is much more than merely a superb technician. He is a big-city pastor with a shepherd's heart, and that gentle touch always communicates to people in the various aspects of his ministry.

It communicates in this book, too. Doctor Walker has a straightforward, no-nonsense style that is as effective on the printed page as it is when he speaks face-to-face. No one cuts to the core of a problem and shines the truth of Scripture on it any better.

I first met Dr. Walker fifteen years ago and have shared with him as a colleague and friend in many situations. His ministry during these years has been the greatest single influence on the development of my own Christian discipleship. But I am not alone in that. He has been to hundreds of young Christians—and those not so young—a compelling spokesman and model for living in the Kingdom. He believes that there *are* answers to life's crises, and his gift for leading others to those answers gives this book a powerful and permanent impact.

CHARLES PAUL CONN, Ph.D.

Preface

In Margaret Mitchell's novel, *Gone with the Wind,* Will delivers an oration at Mr. O'Hara's funeral which sets the context for present-day living. Will says, "Everybody's mainspring is different. And I want to say this—folks whose mainsprings are busted are better dead."

Because we live in a day of stretched, twisted, over-worked, and broken mainsprings, we need strong inner resources that will provide us with courage for crisis living.

Thus, the purpose of this book is to chart a course from Scripture to enhance and enrich the development of these resources to their highest potentiality.

The material in these chapters has been compiled from sermons delivered to the Mount Paran congregation. I am indebted to this family of believers for their enthusiastic support, involved interest, and dedicated discipleship. Each Sunday we experience together the fellowship of the Holy Spirit, out of which these messages have grown.

Deep appreciation is expressed to Jim Pennington, Marshall Thomas, Mary Frances Cowan, Beverly Rogers, Susan Reabold, and others of the Mount Paran Communications Department for their work in editing tapes and providing transcripts for use in the writing process.

A special note of thanks goes to Joy Wooderson, secretary *par excellence,* for her constant encouragement, efficient handling of details, and typing expertise in preparing the manuscript for publication.

An ever-growing love and gratitude are extended to Carmelita, my wife, whose calm spirit, serene style, and deep Christian commitment provide both an impetus for growth and a resource for nurture. In many ways hers is the supreme sacrifice, for she gives to me in order that I may give to others.

1

Courage for Crisis Living

You know, any way we look at it, we have to face a lot of tough questions about living in our world today.

For instance, we ask the question "Has the law of success, the law of expediency, the law of technological triumph replaced the law of moral integrity?"

Everything was going along so well. Success and progress were the orders of the day, and then something happened. Somebody told us that the Lord God of Israel was dead, so we manufactured a lot of new gods for ourselves. For a while the new gods paid off, but now we find ourselves in the position where the new gods are failing us.

The Crises

Oh, it is true that with our new gods we have improved our medical care and nutrition, but in the process we have produced a population crisis.

It is true that with our new gods we have redistributed our population and resettled in the large city centers, but in the process we have produced an urban crisis.

It is true that with our new gods we have increased the gross national product at a phenomenal rate, but in the process we have squandered our natural resources and produced an ecological crisis.

It is true that with our new gods we have learned how to live for the moment and forget about the future. We have learned how to ignore the meaning of sin. We have learned how to defy the laws of the universe. We have learned how to rebel against the commandments of the God of Israel, and we have learned how to violate our own consciences, and in the process we have produced a moral crisis.

And now we ask the question "Who is to blame?" Is it the media—the schools—the churches—the government—the family?

Who started these wretched and interminable wars that keep popping up all over the world? Who ruined our earth, air, and water? Who polluted our beautiful rivers, lakes, and streams? Who misguided our youth, supplied them with drugs, and taught them how to use them? Who corrupted our politics, perverted our politicians, and degraded our judicial system? Who brought us under this kind of bondage so that we find ourselves slaves to the bottle, the pill, and the weed?

We stand back and say, "What's happening? Everything seems to be coming unraveled. Everything seems to be falling apart." Life is one gigantic crisis, and we desperately search for the power to cope.

At some time or other we have all been there. We know the meaning of crisis. We know what it is to hurt.

My telephone rings, and the young lady on the other end of the line says, "Will you please pray for me? Three months ago my father died from a heart attack. Six weeks ago my husband was killed in an automobile accident. I've come to Atlanta to start a new life, and I'm so lonely. I'm so afraid. I'm so full of hurt!"

I read my mail, and a man writes:

You don't know me, but I know you. I sit in your congregation every Sunday night. I'm a man in trouble. I'm a chain smoker, and I've smoked so much, until the doctors tell me that I have cancer. I have to drink every day. If I don't, I get the shakes. I'm an insomniac. I'm just one step from death. I'm barely existing. Can you please help me?

It's only two days until Christmas. We are enjoying a family evening at home. The telephone rings. I listen to my mother's voice from five hundred miles away, "Your dad just died!"

Sure it hurts—it's a crisis—but what do you do? How do you handle it? What a tragedy if there is no answer. What a tragedy if there is no way out. What a tragedy if crisis is the climax and hurt is the finale.

But there is a way out. This is the message of the Bible. *You can have courage for crisis living!* You can take it! Crisis is the overture. Hurt is the introduction. Courage is the climax, and God is the ultimate resource.

This was the message of Job: "Though he [God] slay me, yet will I trust in him . . ." (Job 13:15 KJV). This was the message of David: "Yea, though I walk through the valley of the shadow of death, I will fear no evil: for thou art with me; thy rod and thy staff they comfort me" (Psalms 23:4 KJV). This was the message of Isaiah: "Thou wilt keep him in perfect peace, whose mind is stayed on thee: because he trusteth in thee" (Isaiah 26:3 KJV). This was the message of Paul: "For I am persuaded, that neither death, nor life, nor angels, nor principalities, nor powers, nor things present, nor things to come, Nor height, nor depth, nor any other creature, shall be able to separate us from the love of God, which is in Christ Jesus our Lord" (Romans 8:38, 39 KJV).

But then we back off and say, "Come on now! That sounds great, but how do we really make it work? How do we handle the hurt—the disappointment—the guilt—the fear—the worry—the anxiety—the crisis?"

Sometimes we feel as if there is no way out. Nothing ever seems to work out right. In fact, most of us can identify with the Manhattan businessman who had to catch the Staten Island Ferry every day at 5:00 P.M. to get home at a decent hour in the evening. If he missed it, he wouldn't arrive home until after 9:00 P.M. One Friday he ran late at the office. In a mad rush, he jammed everything in his brief-case, grabbed a taxi, weaved recklessly through the traffic, screeched to a halt on the ferry ramp, saw the ferry about ten feet away from the dock in the water, dashed down the ramp, took one long leap, and barely caught the rail of the boat. He rested a minute, caught his breath, wiped the perspiration off his brow, and said, "Whew, I just barely made it." "Yes, I know," said a bystander, "but this boat is coming in!"

Isn't this our situation at times? We are on an outboat coming in when we really want to be on an inboat going out.

But where is the answer? How can we cope? How can we find courage for crisis living?

The Courage

In a word, the Bible has an answer, and it is God's statement to Joshua: "Be strong and of a good courage . . ." (Joshua 1:6 KJV). Suddenly we find a key. Suddenly we have a formula. ". . . do not be fearful or dismayed, for the Lord your God is with you wherever you go" (v. 9 NEB).

Joshua and Israel were in a crisis. Moses was dead. It was time to cross the Jordan and enter the Promised Land. Israel had to change leadership in the middle of the stream. The nation could have panicked, but God gave a three-step formula for courage in crisis living.

Stake Your Claim

God said to Joshua, "Every place where you set foot is yours: I have given it to you, as I promised Moses" (Joshua 1:3 NEB). In one terse statement God told Joshua to stake his claim. In a very real sense, God says the very same thing to us. "Take Me at My word. Trust Me to perform what I have promised. Pray in faith and expect results!" This is God's courage for crisis living.

Didn't James say, ". . . You do not have, because you do not ask God" (James 4:2 NIV)? Didn't Christ say, "Therefore I tell you, whatever you ask for in prayer, believe that you will receive it, and it will be yours" (Mark 11:24 NIV)?

"Well," you say, "that sounds good, but will it work in the twentieth century?"

It worked for a seventy-year-old woman in California. She had been a widow for several years, lived in a modest home in a town of less than ten thousand people. One night she had a vision that the community needed a nursing home for the aged. She called a meeting of the town's only banker, the leading lawyer, the only contractor, and the mayor. Without wasting any time, she stated her case and said, "The Lord has told me to tell you to loan me the money and do what is necessary to build a nursing home." In as nice a way as they knew how, they each in essence said, "You've got to be kidding. You're out of your mind!"

But six months later I dedicated a new nursing home valued at $150,000. Just before the dedication service, the contractor said, "This is the biggest gamble I ever took." The banker said, "If I get caught making this kind of loan, I could lose my job." The mayor said, "This is poor politics." The lawyer said, "I'm seeing it, but I'm not believing it."

We cut the ribbon, dedicated the building to the glory of God, and in three months' time all the rooms were filled, with a waiting list. It all happened because one seventy-year-old woman dared to stake a claim.

Sort Out Your Faith

God told Joshua, "No one will ever be able to stand against you: as I was with Moses, so will I be with you; I will not fail you or forsake you" (Joshua 1:5 NEB).

This affirmation was all that Joshua needed. God had promised to give him the same protective care and miraculous intervention that He had given Moses. Joshua was ready to meet the enemy head-on.

Isn't this what Jesus had in mind when He said, "I tell you the truth, anyone who has faith in me will do what I have been doing. He will do even greater things than these, because I am going to the Father" (John 14:12 NIV)?

To put it in contemporary terms, Jesus was saying, "Sort out your faith! Put it into gear! Make it work for you!"

An alcoholic friend of mine found out that this is true, "God will be with you; God will not fail you or forsake you," and here is what he writes:

Dear Pastor:

A miracle has taken place in my life. The pain and suffering I brought on myself could not have been completely changed if this were not so.

My addiction had become so great, I was not able to function in speech or normal physical movements. My body shook constantly, and my mind was so twisted I could not make a simple decision. My marriage had fallen apart, and I had lost contact with my children.

For years I had prayed for God's help to overcome my weakness, and for years I felt He had not answered my prayers. Now I know He did answer them. I know now He had to let me go through the horrors and nightmares I have had so that I could understand and appreciate what it means to enjoy the love and peace of mind that can only be found by accepting God as my Saviour.

I finally realized I had failed completely in trying to control my life. I asked God to take over my life because I knew then neither I nor any human being could help me, but that God could and would if I would let Him. The teachings I learned in Christ, and the friendships I made gave me the faith that my life would be changed if I let God have control.

The first few days were not easy, but I saw I could make it one day at a time. Each morning I ask God for strength and help, and at night I thank Him for His protection and guidance.

Life today is great, and I am at peace with myself. My family and friends love me, and I even love myself. When I get upset, I remember to let go and let God take over.

Faith in God will bring miracles.

Your friend,

RUSSELL

It worked for Joshua! It worked for Russell! It will work for you! Sort out your faith: "No one will ever be able to stand against you: as I was with Moses, so will I be with you; I will not fail you or forsake you" (Joshua 1:5 NEB).

Stay in Touch

There is a final step in this plan of courage. God told Joshua to ". . . observe diligently all the law which my servant Moses has given you. You must not turn from it to right or left, if you would prosper wherever you go" (Joshua 1:7 NEB).

This is the plan. If we are going to stake a claim and sort out our faith, we have to meet the conditions of that claim by staying in touch with God's Word: ". . . observe diligently all the law which my servant Moses has given you . . ." (Joshua 1:7 NEB).

Often we say, "I want God's promises, but I don't want to pay the price. I want the Promised Land, but I don't want to go through the wilderness. I want to win the race, but I don't want to run around the track. I want to play in the concert, but I don't want to practice. I want the rewards, but I don't want the discipline of discipleship. I want the courage, but I don't want to live by the plan. I want to do it my way, I don't want to stay in touch."

There is no other way but to stay in close touch with
God's Word. The Bible says we receive our claim when we
come to Him with a contrite heart (*see* 2 Chronicles 7:14).
We receive our claim when we come to Him in faith (*see*
Mark 11:24). We receive our claim when we seek Him with
all our hearts (*see* Jeremiah 29:13). We receive our claim
when we confess our faults and pray for one another, because ". . . The prayer of a righteous man is powerful and
effective" (James 5:16 NIV). We receive our claim when we
truly obey Him, for ". . . if our hearts do not condemn us,
we have confidence before God and receive from him anything we ask, because we obey his commands and do what
pleases him" (1 John 3:21, 22 NIV).

Ginger Jackson found this out. Several years ago she
came into my office with the marks of hardness and care of
the world written in the lines of her face. I would have
guessed her to be in her fifties or sixties. She looked at me
out of eyes of despair, and I'll never forget what she said:
"How old do you think I am?" Well, obviously, I've
learned a long time ago to avoid that question like the
plague. She insisted, so, finally I said, "I think you are in
your fifties." Tears welled up in her eyes, and she said,
"I'm twenty-four." Then, like a mighty flood, the bitterness came pouring forth. Her life was a dirty mess. She
lived the life of a junkie, an alcoholic, and a prostitute. The
needle marks had festered. Her hands shook. Her hair had
been coming out until she was starting to become bald. Her
skin was rough and wrinkled.

Then, almost out of the clear blue, she looked up and
asked, "Do you think that it is too late for God to do anything with old me?"

And this is the marvelous thing about the gospel. God has
been taking "old me's" for centuries and turning them into
"new me's."

In prayer and faith we read Joshua 1 together and followed the formula of courage for crisis living: *Stake the*

claim—sort out your faith—stay in touch! In the office that day, God gave her a new lease on life. This was followed up by hospitalization, therapy, and a new center of life in a fellowship of believers. Within the year she came back to see me, and I hardly recognized her. Now she was truly twenty-four. She looked and acted the part in every way. To use her words, "God gave me the courage, and I have found a miracle life."

This is courage for crisis living, and this is the power of God for you: ". . . do not be fearful or dismayed, for the Lord your God is with you wherever you go" (Joshua 1:9 NEB).

2

The Paradox of Being OK

Have you ever had the experience of wishing that you couldn't feel, because the pain and the suffering were almost too hard to bear? Have you ever had that "ache all over" kind of experience where you felt as if your very insides were being torn apart?

Probably, if we are really honest with ourselves, every one of us at some time or other has been at that place: a terrifying loss—the death of a loved one—unjust treatment by a close friend—a tragic illness—a disappointing hurt because certain plans didn't materialize—being let down in some very desperate circumstances—we have all felt NOT OK.

This must have been the way the Psalmist felt in Psalms 25:16, 17 when he said, "Turn to me and show me thy favor, for I am lonely and oppressed. Relieve the sorrows of my heart and bring me out of my distress" (NEB). This must have been the way he felt in Psalms 31:11, 12, and we hear him cry out, "I have such enemies that all men scorn me: my neighbours find me a burden, my friends shudder at me; when they see me in the street they turn quickly away. I am forgotten, like a dead man out of mind; I have come to be like something lost" (NEB).

This is the way that Pete felt, and here is what he wrote from a motel room somewhere in Arkansas:

Dear Dr. Walker:

I once lived in Atlanta, and much of my spiritual growth came through your words and your church. I never met you, but I attended your church and felt very close to God there.

I'm in trouble now. I desperately need your prayers. I've all but lost my faith. I'm struggling in sin. I'm lost. I've lost the ability to love. I'm a wreck. I'm very talented in the eyes of the world, but I'm wasting all of my talents I once thought God had given me. I don't do anything anymore. I'm lazy. I sleep when I can to try to forget about my life.

I need your prayers, and I need to feel forgiven. I need to love and be loved. I need my faith in God and a faith in tomorrow. Please pray for me. I constantly think of myself and my troubles. I want to love people again.

I'm closing now with a prayer. I am lost.

PETE

In our own ways we each can identify with Pete, but this is not really the way we want it. The truth is that we would really like to have the kind of life-style that makes us know that we are OK. We would really like to have the position in life whereby we can satisfy our needs in a socially acceptable and responsible way. We would really like to be able to act in keeping with our value systems and basic chronological ages. We would really like to behave in ways that would be appropriate to the situations in which we find ourselves. We would really like to come off with social presence, social poise, and a sense of social power, regardless of the circumstances. We would really like to face up to the problems of life and meet them with mastery.

In a word, we would like to look at ourselves and say—I'M OK! I have freedom of choice—freedom to change—freedom to find purpose, meaning, and direction for my life.

The Paradox

In reality this is the good news of the gospel—YOU CAN BE OK! And when the Bible talks about an OK life, it talks in terms of a brand-new style and formulates it in a *paradox*—a power contrary to received opinion, an assertion contrary to common notion. In fact, Christ says that the paradox of being OK is that you must be born again! This was His message to Nicodemus: ". . . I tell you the truth, unless a man is born again, he cannot see the kingdom of God" (John 3:3 NIV). Like many of us, Nicodemus had a problem handling such a strange statement; so he asked the obvious question, ". . . how can a man be born when he is old? Surely he cannot enter a second time into his mother's womb to be born!" (John 3:4 NIV). In turn, Jesus laid out the paradox again ". . . I tell you the truth, unless a man is born of water and the Spirit, he cannot enter the kingdom of God" (John 3:5 NIV).

But then we look around at our circumstances and say to ourselves, "You've got to be kidding! Be born again! Start all over brand-new! You don't know what I've been through! As far as I am concerned, God has abandoned me. I can no longer trust Him to fulfill my needs. God is unable. God is unwilling. God is unaware. I must be doing something wrong, or certainly I wouldn't be in this mess I am in!"

But the truth is that there is good news in spite of the circumstances, and this good news is that God is able. God is willing. God is aware.

The Principle

The Psalmist had to learn this, too. The same Psalmist who said, "I am lonely and oppressed," the same Psalmist who said, "My friends shudder at me . . . I am forgotten like a dead man" found the paradox of being OK, and we hear him proclaiming a whole new principle of living in

Psalms 139:6: "This is too glorious, too wonderful to believe! I can never be lost to your Spirit! I can never get away from my God. If I go up to heaven, you are there; if I go down to the place of the dead, you are there. If I ride the morning winds to the farthest oceans, even there your hand will guide me, your strength will support me. If I try to hide in the darkness, the night becomes light around me" (LB).

And what about the message of the prophet? "Although the fig-tree does not burgeon, the vines bear no fruit, the olive-crop fails, the orchards yield no food, the fold is bereft of its flock and there are no cattle in the stalls, yet I will exult in the Lord and rejoice in the God of my deliverance" (Habakkuk 3:17 NEB).

Do you remember the words of Christ? "Until now you have not asked for anything in my name. Ask and you will receive, and your joy will be complete" (John 16:24 NIV).

Then what about the dynamic power of living illustrated by the apostle Paul? What a paradox of being OK!

> Called "imposters" we must be true, called "nobodies" we must be in the public eye. Never far from death, yet here we are alive, always "going through it" yet never "going under." We know sorrow, yet our joy is inextinguishable. We have "nothing to bless ourselves with" yet we bless many others with true riches. We are penniless, and yet in reality we have everything worth having.
>
> 2 Corinthians 6:8–10 PHILLIPS

"Sounds great," we say, "but what about right here in the twentieth century? Can I become OK right now?"

Well, Chris did, and here is what happened to her:

Dear Pastor Paul:

I have to let you know that my life is just beginning at twenty-four. I'm a brand-new person; I'm overwhelmed with the HOLY SPIRIT!

Depression, compulsive overeating and suicidal thoughts have plagued me for eight long and miserable years. I've been to psychiatrists, and I've been in hospitals, but there is no hospital like the power of the Holy Spirit. My life has taken a 360 degree turn! My heart overflows with love and happiness. Time no longer hangs heavy on my shoulders. Time is precious now, for I have so much to do and so much joy to spread . . . .

I'm so blessed to be living in this glorious world. While walking this morning, I saw five beautiful bluebirds flying one right after the other. I praised the Lord for allowing me to see such a thrilling sight. This world is full of beauty for all those who are willing to look for it!

Your loving friend,

CHRIS

The Power

So how do we get to that? It's a valid question, and there is a valid answer. Paul the apostle found it and expressed it in Philippians 3:13, 14: ". . . Forgetting what is behind and straining toward what is ahead, I press on toward the goal to win the prize for which God has called me heavenward in Christ Jesus" (NIV).

Now we have to ask ourselves, "What does all this mean when it comes to being OK?"

First, TO BECOME OK WE HAVE TO FORGET THE PAST. Paul says it loud and clear, ". . . Forgetting what is behind . . . ."

Isn't this one of our primary problems today—dealing with our pasts? Sometimes we drag them around as if they were long-lost friends. Every activity, every attitude, every feeling, every decision, and practically every thought are influenced by the past.

Paul could have become a bitter man. Look at what he suffered!

I have been beaten times without number.
I have faced death again and again.
I have been beaten the regulation thirty-nine stripes by the Jews five times.
I have been beaten with rods three times.
I have been stoned once.
I have been shipwrecked three times.
I have been twenty-four hours in the open sea.
In my travels I have been in constant danger from rivers, and floods, from bandits, from my own countrymen, and from pagans. I have faced danger in city streets, danger in the desert, danger on the high seas, danger among false Christians. I have known exhaustion, pain, long vigils, hunger and thirst, doing without meals, cold and lack of clothing.

2 Corinthians 11:23–27 PHILLIPS

There was every reason for Paul to NOT BE OK—every reason to be hung up on a terrible past—but something happened to Paul. He had a living encounter with a living God, which resulted in a new power for living: "if anyone is in Christ, he is a new creation; the old has gone, the new has come!" (2 Corinthians 5:17 NIV). Paul was able to forget the past and learn that he could do everything through Christ, who gave him strength (*see* Philippians 4:13). Paul found the paradox of being OK.

Second, TO BECOME OK WE HAVE TO FACE UP TO THE FUTURE. In Philippians 3:13, Paul said, "I'm straining toward what is ahead . . . ." The Phillips rendering is, ". . . with hands outstretched to whatever lies ahead I go straight for the goal . . . ."

Obviously, there is no way to face the future if we take our past with us. If we push the same buttons of the past, our future will be just like our past. If we persist in the same attitudes of the past, our future will be just like our past. If we play the same mental tapes of the past that tell us we are NOT OK, our future will still be NOT OK.

To face up to the future, we have to have a fresh spiritual and mental attitude. Like Paul, we must fix our minds on ". . . things which are holy and right and pure and beautiful and good" (Philippians 4:8 PHILLIPS).

It really means that we need the attitude of the man who was in his late seventies; he had such an enthusiastic and effervescent spirit that everyone who knew him marveled at his exuberance. One day somebody asked him, "What is the secret of your joyous life-style? How is it that you have such a positive attitude about the future?" Without hesitation he replied, "It's really very simple. The answer is in the Bible." The inquirer responded, "You found it in the Bible? Where is it in the Bible?" Again, without a hitch, the old man said, "Well the Bible says, 'It came to pass,' but nowhere does it say that it came to stay."

Any way we look at it, the pressures of life are temporary. Our problems are not here to stay. How did the Psalmist put it? "Tears may linger at nightfall, but joy comes in the morning" (Psalms 30:5 NEB).

The future is not in the headlines of the newspaper. The future is not on the six and eleven o'clock newscasts. The future is not in Washington, Moscow, Peking, or the UN. The future is found in the hands of a loving God who writes our destiny in His living Word with the eternal promise of a day when ". . . God himself will be with them [His people] and be their God. He will wipe every tear from their eyes. There will be no more death or mourning or crying or pain, for the old order of things has passed away" (Revelation 21:3, 4 NIV).

This is the paradox of being OK: ". . . the old order of things has passed away."

But there is another dimension to consider: TO BECOME

OK WE HAVE TO PRESS FOR THE PRESENT.

Paul said, "I press on toward the goal . . ." (Philippians 3:14 NIV). But what does it mean "to press"? Actually it is a very important phrase that we use in many different ways. "To press" is to push as you push a button. "To press" is to exert pressure such as pressing or ironing clothes. "To press" is to make a great exertion as the weightlifter does when he "snatches" and "presses" several hundred pounds above his head. "To press" is to gamble, and it means to go for broke. "To press" is to relentlessly pursue or intensely go after.

So, in reality, Paul is saying, I push; I exert; I go for broke; I relentlessly pursue the present moment and make it count for the goal of Christ.

The truth is that we only have the "now." The past is gone; the future is ahead; what we have is this present moment in time.

Maybe that's why Beethoven was such an effective composer. He stretched his lifetime to its fullest extent. He was so far ahead of his time that his biographer observed, "Beethoven gave creations that were far beyond the contemporary means of expression." He composed music that the existing instruments couldn't play. As a result, Beethoven forced new techniques to be developed and caused new instruments to be formed. Beethoven pressed for the present. He became OK, and even while suffering from deafness, created the beautiful Ninth Symphony that stands as a classic of all times.

You see, God didn't create instruments to play music. God created music for instruments to play. And this is what God wants to do for us. He wants us to become the kind of instruments that can play the music of the creative power of being OK.

This is the paradox of being OK. You can be born again— *forget the past—face up to the future —press for the present.*

3

Will the Real You
Please Stand Up!

In our world today we have learned how to do many
important things. We have learned how to use a needle and
a piece of wax to preserve sound for centuries. We have
learned how to make a crystal and a piece of wire send
sound around the world. We have learned how to take a
scalpel and the trained hand of a surgeon to operate between the beats of a heart. We have learned how to utilize a
picture tube and a sound wave to put a television picture in
practically every home. We have learned how to make use
of a jet thrust and a rocket to enable us to travel to the
moon.

But in all of this, we have never learned how to live life
with mastery—to meet life on its own terms—to cope with
life regardless—to be content whatever the situation.

If we stop to ask ourselves, "What kind of persons do we
really want to be?" How would we answer?

Obviously there would be a variety of responses, but
most of us would say, "If I could just find a life-style that
would bring healthy and well-adjusted living."

You know, "If I could just be a person of self-
understanding; if I could know my weaknesses, my
strengths, my motives, and my desires; if I could just get
oriented to my environment and understand the forces I
have to deal with every day; if I could become more objective, face facts as they really are, and evaluate my expe-

riences realistically—then my life would make more sense!"

Or, "If I could have more initiative, be more active, really try to solve my problems and quit hesitating; if I could just stop allowing tension and anxiety to inhibit and immobilize me; if I could be more flexible, try to understand others, and truly learn when to give in and when to be firm—then life would have a lot more meaning!"

Or, "If I could become more self-reliant, more confident, and see my problems as occasions for solutions rather than worry; if I could just be optimistic, friendlier, and find more satisfaction in my work, my home, and my family—then life would really come alive!"

If. . . if. . . if . . . and the beat goes on! Sometimes we get so down on ourselves that we lose our identities. We are not sure who we are anymore. In many ways we can probably identify with the rock-and-roll song:

> I'm a gambler; I'm a runner
> But you knew that, when you laid down.
> I'm a picture of ugly stories,
> I'm a killer and I'm a clown.
>
> From *Desperado*
> Alice Cooper and Michael Booth

An ugly story! A killer! A clown! Not a very bright prospect, but too often it accurately describes the defeated life many experience.

This was the case of Lisa. She called me one afternoon. Her voice was faint, her speech was slurred, and she whispered that she was committing suicide from an overdose of drugs. Faintly I heard an address and wrote it down. Then there was silence.

I called the suicide squad, gave them the address, jumped in my car, and rushed to find the apartment. To my dismay there was no such address. Inquiries brought no results, and I returned home frustrated and defeated after a two-hour search.

Two days later a policewoman called to inform me that they had found the dead body of a girl in an apartment. She held a letter that was addressed to me in her hand. Evidently she had attended our church and called me as a last resort. Tragically, it was too late. Here is her letter:

Doctor Walker,
It's four-thirty in the morning. I can't stand living any longer. Inside of me I'm lost and empty. There's so much fear and uncertainty, and a loneliness that never leaves me alone. I don't know what to do. I am so confused. I've got to get away from it all.
I want to live and be happy. I want to be free. I want to love myself and other people. I want my life to have meaning and purpose. I want to be able to look forward to the next day of living and to have peace inside me instead of fear and loneliness. I want the emptiness inside me to be filled with love and happiness. I want to be able to feel the rain and sunshine and hear the birds sing—see the green trees and bright flowers. I want to care for other people and make them happy—love the whole world. I want to be really turned on. I want to smile. I want to live. The question is, *how?*
But it's too late. I've blown my mind too many times. I've tripped out too many times. I've escaped from reality so long that I'm not sure what reality is. I feel like I'm losing my mind, breaking into millions of pieces, and floating into space in thousands of different directions. I try to reach out and put the pieces back together. But I can't catch them, they float away so fast. I'm coming apart. And I know I'll never be able to put the pieces back together again.

LISA

In the policewoman's handwriting, Lisa's description was enclosed:

18 years of age (very pretty)
5'2"
100–110 lbs.
Black hair (long)
Dark brown eyes
Cause of death—overdose of barbiturates—suicide
Dead on arrival
Parents do not want body

The police department located her parents. Lisa lived in San Francisco and ran away from home when she was fifteen. She had not contacted her parents in over two years. In the interim, her parents divorced. Neither one wanted the body for burial.

But God did not create us to be pictures, ugly stories, killers, and clowns. God did not create us to overdose with drugs and commit suicide. God created us in His own image and offers us the resources to achieve our highest potentialities and capabilities. In fact, the whole point of the good news of the gospel is to challenge us with the statement "will the real you please stand up!"

This is what the Psalmist meant when he said, ". . . I am fearfully and wonderfully made . . ." (Psalms 139:14 KJV). This is what the apostle Paul meant when he told us to ". . . put on the new nature (the regenerate self) created in God's image, (Godlike) in true righteousness and holiness" (Ephesians 4:24 AMPLIFIED). This is the message of Psalms 8:4, 5, "What is man, that thou art mindful of him? and the son of man, that thou visitest him? For thou hast made him a little lower than the angels, and hast crowned him with glory and honour" (KJV).

"Fearfully and wonderfully made—crowned with glory and honor—created in God's image"—sounds incredible, doesn't it!

How do we get to that? How does the real "you" stand up?

Like the airline's commercial says, "You gotta believe!"
But what do we believe? Three things: *You are incompara-*
ble! You are invisible! You are invincible!

You Are Incomparable

This is the starting point: "fearfully and wonderfully
made." In fact, each of us is a six-million-dollar person.
Research shows that if the raw materials of the body, such
as the amino acids, the enzymes, the proteins, the hormones, DNA, RNA, and the other biochemicals were to be
evaluated, each person would be worth six million dollars.

Further, if it were possible for human ingenuity to con-
struct these raw materials into living cells, the cost would
be something like 300 trillion dollars. Finally, if we had the
know-how to amass these living cells into a functional
human being, there would not be enough monetary resources in the world to fund the project.

The point is that each of us is a unique individual in the
sight of God. As Christ pointed out, we are the most valuable masterpiece of God's creation; therefore, we are not to
worry about tomorrow, ". . . for tomorrow will worry
about itself. Each day has enough trouble of its own"
(Matthew 6:34 NIV).

We are incomparable! This is God's message to us. This
is why God has given us eyes that can see the sun, about 93
million miles away, and yet can so intricately focus that we
can thread the infinitesimal eye of a needle. He has given us
hands so powerful that we can plow a straight furrow and
yet have the dexterity to operate between the beats of a
heart. He has given us ears that are so delicate that if we
were in a soundproof room, we could hear the very blood
run though our veins. He has given us a heart so strong that
it can pump over fifteen gallons of blood per hour and beat
over 40 million times in a year. He has given us feet that are
so architecturally perfect that the body, regardless of its
weight, is balanced on four small bones the size of a little

finger. He has given us a brain that is so complex that it contains over 10 billion cells and has the capacity to send impulses through the nervous system at the rate of over three hundred fifty feet per second.

Marvelous! Complex! We are the masterpieces of God, and He wants us to use our bodies for His glory. This is why the apostle Paul says, "Do you not know that your body is a temple of the Holy Spirit, who is in you, whom you have received from God? You are not your own; you were bought at a price. Therefore honor God with your body" (1 Corinthians 6:19 NIV).

Tremendous things can happen when we really accept the fact that we are incomparable and become willing to turn our lives over to God. For instance, I once listened to a man speak who had a rich voice that literally filled up the building. The miraculous thing was that he wasn't endowed with a beautiful voice. When he was a boy, he was a stutterer. People made fun of him, and the other kids would taunt him to the point where he would try to defend himself verbally, get all tangled up, and then break into embarrassed tears. At night he would cry himself to sleep and pray to die so he wouldn't have to face his handicap another day.

One day he listened to a senator speak in a YMCA meeting. The senator told the group that through faith in God anything could be accomplished. This impressed the stuttering boy. He thought, "If I pray through faith in God, I wonder if I can overcome my stuttering?" He began to try prayer. His mother saw what was happening and got worried. She had a talk with her son and said, "If you are going to lick this problem, here are two principles you must learn—faith and patience. Keep your patience and give God a chance."

He read about Demosthenes, the Greek orator who improved his speech by putting pebbles in his mouth and practicing his oration. It seemed like a good idea; so he tried it on the shores of Lake Michigan. He would holler to the wind, make speeches to the lake, and soon began to feel very close to God as he prayed and practiced with pebbles in his mouth. He learned to relax and feel the presence of God giving him strength. His stuttering diminished; his speech improved; and in a few months it was as though he had never stuttered.

His name is Al Haake. Later he became the mayor of Park Ridge, Illinois, and one of the most sought-after speakers in the country. If we were to hear him today, we would not be aware he ever stuttered.

Al Haake learned that he was "fearfully and wonderfully made." He also learned that God would give him the power to be incomparable.

In his words, "If God could heal me of my stuttering, he could heal anybody of anything."

You Are Invisible

The body is a masterpiece, but there is more to us than just the exterior. The real "you" is invisible. In fact, it is what's inside that really counts. So what is inside us? If we took a long, hard look, what would we find?

Obviously, there would be a physical self. We would find a skeleton of some 206 bones so perfectly rigged and balanced that through a system of hinges and joints we can run, jump, bend, and absorb shock up to twenty thousand pounds of pressure per square inch. We would find six hundred or more muscles that contract, expand, and pull on the bones to make all types of motion possible. We would discover a circulation network comprising sixty thousand miles of tubing, designed to carry blood to every part of our bodies through a system of arteries, veins and capillaries. We would find a nervous system, a respiratory system, a digestive system, and other functions that provide the capacity to think, coordinate, breathe, and perform the vital activities that maintain life.

But there is far more! Inside us there is also a spiritual

self. It is the world of awareness, the world of experience, the world that desperately needs communication with God.

A beautiful rose attracts our attention. We notice the color, the smell, the feel of the thorns, and the texture of the petals. We form an impression of the rose in our minds. This impression joins past impressions to formulate what we term *experience*. In the same way, we form many impressions inside our minds and hearts to the hundreds of events and situations we meet every day in our outside world. The important thing is that the way in which we make these impressions determines how we behave and what kind of persons we become.

You see, deep inside ourselves we formulate ideas about God, our world, and ourselves. This is where "the fat gets in the fire." These ideas—right, wrong, or indifferent— form our spiritual selves and guide the course of our living. If these ideas are irrational, we live irrational lives. If these ideas are clouded by fantasy, we live unrealistic lives. If these ideas are colored by bitterness, resentment, and self-pity, we live depressed lives.

On the other hand, if these ideas are objective, oriented, aware, flexible, and harmonious, we live balanced lives. If these ideas are empathetic, congruent, respectful, and consistent, we live happy lives in healthy relationships with others. If these ideas are centered on God, imbedded in Christ, and based on His Word, we live productive lives in harmony with the Spirit as the source and center of our being.

This is what Genesis 1:26 means when the Word assures us that we are made in His own image. This is what 1 Peter 3:4 means when we are admonished to emphasize ". . . your inner self, the unfading beauty of a gentle and quiet spirit, which is of great worth in God's sight" (NIV). This is what 2 Corinthians 3:18 means when it emphatically states: "But all of us who are Christians have no veils on our faces, but reflect like mirrors the glory of the Lord. We are transfigured by the Spirit of the Lord in ever-increasing splendour into His own image'' (PHILLIPS).

The point is—the real ''you'' stands up on the inside. We are invisible!

We are character—traits and aspects of behavior to which we attach a definite social and spiritual value. We are adjustment—behavior patterns that enable us to function in social and spiritual settings. We are temperament— variations in energy level, prevailing mood, and general style of life. We are interests—variety of choice in daily activities of work, recreation, and responsibilities. We are attitudes—differences of response and mind set toward groups, institutions, ideas, values, and all aspects of our world.

The key is turning our inside self over to God and forging out a character, molding an adjustment style, developing productive interests, and fashioning positive attitudes:

> [That it might develop] until we all attain oneness in the faith and in the comprehension of the full and accurate knowledge of the Son of God; that [we might arrive] at really mature manhood—the completeness of personality which is nothing less than the standard height of Christ's own perfection—the measure of the stature of the fullness of the Christ, and the completeness found in Him.
>
> Ephesians 4:13 AMPLIFIED

Perhaps it is best illustrated by an incident in the life of Mendelssohn, the great musician, organist, and composer. One day this great master visited a famous cathedral in Europe which had just installed a new organ, reputed to be the best in the world. Mendelssohn naturally wanted to play this magnificent instrument and sought permission from the cathedral organ master, who was practicing. Not recognizing Mendelssohn, the organ master refused but after a few minutes of conversation perceived that Mendelssohn had a vast knowledge of music and organs. Reluctantly he agreed for the master to play "just for thirty seconds."

Mendelssohn sat down, put his talented fingers to the keys, and soon the cathedral was filled with music beyond comparison. The organ master was stunned and immediately recognized both the composition being played and the composer. Chagrined, he cried out in embarrassment, "O my God, the master is here, and I was reluctant to let him play the organ."

God has given us the capacity to produce beautiful inner harmonies, but only when we give the keyboard of our lives to Him can we respond in the fullest capacity of our creative ability.

You Are Invincible

But what happens when we truly give our bodies and our inner spirits to God? What really takes place when we ". . . put on the new nature (the regenerate self) created in God's image . . ." (Ephesians 4:24 AMPLIFIED)? The answer is that we are then prepared to live as we are ". . . a little lower than the angels . . ." and have been ". . . crowned with glory and honour" (Psalms 8:5 KJV).

In short, we are invincible! We can meet life head-on! We can take it regardless!

Thomas Edison demonstrated this. It took ten thousand experiments to perfect the light bulb, but he never gave up. Then, on the night of December 9, 1914, Thomas Edison watched his two-million-dollar plant go up in smoke. He had been assured that it was fireproof, which meant it was only insured for $238,000. Most of us would have been emotionally, physically, and spiritually devastated at such a loss, but not Edison! The next morning, while walking about the charred remains of all his hopes and dreams, Edison was heard to say, "There is great value in disaster. All our mistakes are burned up. Thank God we can start anew."

Only three weeks after the fire, Edison Industries delivered the first phonograph. The real "you" stood up! Edison learned how to be invincible.

The Wells family learned this. They are a close-knit group of one son and three daughters. Then, one day, tragedy struck. Twenty-one-year-old Pam, an experienced hiker and outdoorsman, was killed in a tragic flash flood while hiking and camping with a national hiking club in Texas. As a pastor, I had observed Pam's spiritual development and remember when she shared a part of her diary during one of our many conversations. This is what she wrote:

> I am writing this right after my psychology class. I feel the love of Jesus all over my spirit. I feel energetic, gay, happy, and free. This feeling is probably due to the fact that I've just talked to another believer in Christ. The unity and communion of the Holy Spirit between two believers is so fantastic—WOW!

Just a few short weeks later Pam was taken from us in a freak accident. I was traveling in the Pacific and Japan for the air force when it happened. Upon my return I received a letter from her father. Here is his testimony of invincible faith:

> An interesting thing happened while you were out of town last week. We found the Lord sustaining us by His Spirit working through the Mount Paran ministerial staff and family in a most unusual way. Pam's death, of course, leaves us with a deep sense of personal loss. Our immediate response to the telephone call from West Texas was, "Lord, give her back, please—she's only twenty-one!"
>
> But we found out on our knees at the foot of the cross, some hours later, that His thoughts are far above

our thoughts and His will beyond our will, and in His perfect will He had called her home. So in the following early morning hours we released Pam into the arms of Jesus Christ. It's not easy, but then, He didn't promise us a garden of roses. What He has done staggers and boggles the mind. Imagine! Eternal life beyond the grave! Truly no victory in the grave and no sting in death! Instead, a hallelujah chorus singing "To God Be the Glory!"

Yes, it's true. He's given us His assurance in His Word that He never forsakes us, even in our darkest hour and at the point of physical death. This assurance is undergirded by the fellowship of Christian brothers and sisters everywhere. We find this fellowship especially in our church.

Pam's greeting to the Master likely is embodied in the second stanza of the hymn on page ninety-three of the church hymnal. Truly, "The Comforter Has Come," and He proclaims to all the universe that He has gained the victory over Satan, the enemy, and death.

For the Wells family the real "you"—the invincible "you"—stood up. It can happen in each of our lives. We are made out of tough stuff. When the real "you" stands up in the redeeming, sustaining power of God, you are incomparable! You are invisible! You are invincible!

4

From Fractured Feelings
to a Functional Faith

It was night in an upper room in Jerusalem. The disciples had gathered for the last supper with their Master, Jesus Christ. The Passover Feast was completed. The thanksgiving song had ended. The lamps in the tents had gone out, and the lights that dotted the sides of Mount Olivet had been extinguished. The tramp of feet and the sound of voices had long since ceased. The crowded city streets were empty, and there was a great calmness in the city.

The Roman sentinels on the walls paced back and forth silently, as though they had been called to guard the city of the dead. It was almost midnight, and Jesus Christ looked at His disciples and spoke. As He broke the silence and interrupted the quietness, the disciples hung on every word. Their hearts were filled with love, compassion, and tenderness. After all, at this very moment they could sense His burden. If necessary, they would be persecuted with Him. They would suffer with Him. They would die with Him.

Then Jesus told them some things that really shook them up: ". . . This very night you will all fall away on account of me, for it is written: 'I will strike the shepherd, and the sheep of the flock will be scattered.' But after I have risen, I will go ahead of you into Galilee" (Matthew 26:31, 32 NIV).

Simon Peter couldn't fathom such statements. This was

incredulous, preposterous, ridiculous! How could He talk like this? "Even if all fall away on account of You, I never will," was Peter's response. (*See* Matthew 26:33.)

Christ looked at him with sadness in His eyes. With sorrow in His voice, Christ answered:

"I tell you the truth . . . this very night, before the rooster crows, you will disown me three times." But Peter declared, "Even if I have to die with you, I will never disown you." And all the other disciples said the same.

Matthew 26:34, 35 NIV

"We will never deny you!" This was the theme, but the scene drastically shifts, and by verse fifty-eight the attitude has changed. "But Peter followed him at a distance, right up to the courtyard of the high priest. He entered and sat down with the guards to see the outcome" (Matthew 26:58 NIV). Peter sat in the gallery and watched while the mob accused Christ of blasphemy and cried out for His very life: "He is worthy of death!" They spit in His face, struck Him with their fists, slapped Him, and mocked Him with such taunting phrases as, "Prophesy to us, Christ. Who hit you?" (*See* Matthew 26:65–67.)

Peter had a box seat to watch the unfolding drama, but as he sat there in the palace a servant girl came and said, "You also were with Jesus of Galilee." Peter turned pale and felt his stomach churn.

Defensively, he denied it before them all. "I don't know what you're talking about," he said. Peter walked out on the porch, and another girl spied him and said to the people, "This fellow was with Jesus of Nazareth." The pressure was rising, and with an oath Peter denied it again and emphatically stated, "I don't know the man!" After a while, some of those standing around went up to Peter and said, "Surely you are one of them, for your accent gives you away." It was almost more than he could bear. In a frenzy, Peter called down curses on himself and swore to them, "I don't know the man!" (*See* Matthew 26:67–74.)

In the distance, a rooster crowed. "Then Peter remembered the word Jesus had spoken: 'Before the rooster crows, you will disown me three times.' And he went outside and wept bitterly" (Matthew 26:75 NIV).

Peter fell apart! *His feelings were fractured.* His purpose was lost. His meaning for living was gone, and he was burdened with guilt. "When I was needed the most, I couldn't come through. What I said I wouldn't do is exactly what I'm doing. Where I thought I was strong, I'm weak. Where I thought I had power, I have nothing." These may have been his thoughts.

In the same vein, a lady came into my office and said, "For thirty years I've held it all together. For thirty years I've had power and strength enough to keep from falling apart, but this morning my husband said he wants a divorce. After thirty years of marriage, he's leaving me. I can't stand it anymore." Her body was racked with sobs, and her feelings were fractured.

I walk into a restaurant to eat lunch. A man comes out of the lounge, follows me to my table, and says, "Are you Dr. Walker?" We introduce ourselves, and then he says, "I don't really know you. I've been to your church a couple of times. I'm not a member of your congregation or any congregation, but I'm falling apart. After twenty years on my job, I was fired this morning. I'm fifty-five years old. I don't know where to turn. I've got to go home and tell my wife and children I no longer have a job to support them. I've been drinking for the last two hours, trying to get up the courage. I'm going to pieces. Maybe I should commit suicide. At least there would be the insurance." His feelings were fractured.

We've all been there, haven't we? We go out and weep bitterly because when we were needed the most, we copped out. When we reached back to use our reserves, we just didn't have them. Like Peter, we go on a guilt trip. We suffer an accusative sense of failure. We assume unrealistic responsibility for tragic circumstances and allow our imaginations to burden us with overreaction and undue blame.

Sometimes we feel like Judas, "I've sinned and betrayed innocent blood." (*See* Matthew 27:4.) Sometimes we feel like the brothers of Joseph, "We are guilty concerning our brother because we didn't hear the anguish of his heart. We paid no attention, and now is this distress come upon us." (*See* Genesis 42:21.) Sometimes we feel like David, and we say to ourselves, "I feel like a pelican in the wilderness . . . an owl in the desert . . . a sparrow on a housetop." (*See* Psalms 102.) Our feelings are fractured, and we are not sure what to do.

What are we going to do? Where are we going to go? These were the questions the disciples had to face. Then came the Resurrection, with the startling appearances of Christ: but the feelings were still unresolved, the ambivalence still persisted, the gnawing sense of guilt was still knotted in the stomach.

Peter had had it! In an impulsive moment he said, "I'm going out to fish." The other disciples with him shared his feeling. "So they went out and got into the boat, but that night they caught nothing" (*see* John 21:1–3). From bad to worse! The death of Christ! A strange resurrection! Puzzling appearances! And now—no fish! How much worse could things really be?

A shadowy figure appeared on the beach. The disciples looked up in the dim morning light. A voice came cutting through the morning fog:

". . . Friends, haven't you caught any fish?"

"No," they answered.

He said, "Throw your net on the right side of the boat and you will find some." When they did, they were unable to haul the net in because of the large number of fish.

Then the disciple whom Jesus loved said to Peter, "It is the Lord! . . ."

John 21:5–7 NIV

Impulsive as ever, Peter loses his cool. ". . . As soon as Simon Peter heard him say, 'It is the Lord,' he wrapped his outer garment around him (for he had taken it off) and jumped into the water" (John 21:7 NIV).

Strange as this may seem, it was the beginning of a functional faith. In this encounter a whole new era of discipleship began. The disciples moved from fractured feelings to a functional faith.

Accent Your Faith

First this move meant an accent on faith. "It is the Lord!" This is the starting point. When everything else fails, what do we need more than anything else? "It is the Lord!" When the psychiatrist hasn't helped; the hospitals haven't helped; the doctors haven't helped; the advice of friends hasn't helped; the reading hasn't helped; the church hasn't helped; and we've tried everything imaginable. What is the answer? "It is the Lord!"

Isn't our problem that we don't recognize Him when He really comes? We expect Him in such stereotyped ways. We always want Him in greatness. We want Him in power. We want Him in the gigantic, the colossal, the miraculous, and the stupendous. But most of the time He does not come in clouds, chariots, and armies. When His people need Him the most, He stands there on the beach and says, "Children! It is the Lord!"

And this should be enough! Faith simply says I commit my ways into the hands of the Lord. He is faithful to help me work it out.

A pastor's wife found this out, and here is what she says:

. . . There are times when I give my husband a rough time verbally and hurt him. I end up hating myself and wanting to take my life. Yesterday I was ready to finish off about forty Valium pills when I decided to turn on your program and do the dishes while I contemplated what I was going to do.

Being a pastor's wife, I find my feelings difficult to cope with at times. I've had a lot of adjusting to do in the past year, and Satan has really had a good time with my weak points.

Faith has been my biggest struggle. Now I'm beginning to say to God, "It's in Your hands (whatever the problem may be) and I need Your help, God, to leave it in Your hands so that You can do something with it and me."

From fractured feelings to a functional faith, "I'm beginning to say to God, 'It's in your hands . . . .' "

Accept Your Opportunities

It wasn't easy for Peter. There was a lot of "crow" to eat. Look at all the stupid statements he had made. But Christ gave him a new opportunity. When they finally got ashore, Christ said to them, "Come and have breakfast." The King James Version says, "Come and dine" (John 21:12).

This was like music to their ears. The relationship was still intact. They were going to have another opportunity to sit with Him for a meal. The last one had been a disaster. They had all struck out! Now it was a new day. They could accept new opportunities.

Maybe the most important lesson we can learn from this is that failure is not final. It is only temporary, and the most important thing in life is to make the most of new opportunities.

We are so quick to accept failure, but there is hope for a

new start. For instance, there was a young army officer who surrendered to the enemy in the French and Indian War. Later he became the Father of Our Country. His name was George Washington. He made the most of his opportunities.

There was a man who failed in business. Later he was defeated for the legislature, defeated for elector, defeated for the congress, defeated for the senate and defeated for the vice presidency. However, in 1860 he was elected as President of the United States, and his efforts brought the Emancipation Proclamation. His name was Abraham Lincoln. He made the most of his opportunities.

Walt Disney was told by the *Kansas City Star* that he should give up art and try a different profession. In fact, his first cartoon character, Oswald the rabbit, was classified a failure. Then there came Mickey Mouse, Donald Duck, Disney World, and all the rest. He made the most of his opportunities.

Otis was a failure as an automobile mechanic. Then he invented the elevator. Many of us ride one of his creations every day. The next time we pass the fortieth floor in the building where we work maybe we should say, "This elevator was built by a failure." Not true! Otis made the most of his opportunities.

This is the route to a functional faith. "Come and dine." Accept the new opportunity to utilize the power of Jesus Christ.

Actualize Your Calling

Breakfast is over. Jesus turns to Simon Peter:

". . . Simon son of John, do you truly love me more than these?"

"Yes, Lord," he said, "you know that I love you."

Jesus said, "Feed my lambs."

Again Jesus said, "Simon son of John, do you truly love me?"

He answered, "Yes, Lord, you know that I love you."

Jesus said, "Take care of my sheep."

The third time he said to him, "Simon son of John, do you love me?"

Peter was hurt because Jesus asked him the third time, "Do you love me?" He said, "Lord, you know all things; you know that I love you."

Jesus said, "Feed my sheep."

John 21:15–17 NIV

Powerful dialogue, isn't it? Christ gave Simon Peter a personal commission. In a very real way, Christ gives each one of us a personal commission. He confronts us with discipleship and calls us to follow Him. But what does it mean to follow Him? How do we really affirm our calling?

Well, there is a way of cheap grace. Dietrich Bonhoeffer, the modern Christian martyr, made that clear when he wrote about grace from his Nazi prison cell.

Cheap grace is sold on the market like cheap goods. It is grace as a general system without justification of the sinner, without repentance, without discipline, without confession, without the cross, and without the lordship of Jesus Christ.

On the other hand, there is costly grace. It is selling all that we have to buy the treasure that is hidden in the field. It is liquidating all of our holdings to purchase the pearl of great price. It is accepting the kingly rule of Christ to the point where we will divest ourselves of everything that is unlike Christ. In biblical language, "If your right eye causes you to sin, gouge it out and throw it away . . . . And if your right hand causes you to sin, cut it off and throw it away. It is better for you to lose one part of your body than for your whole body to go into hell" (Matthew 5:29, 30 NIV).

This is a functional faith that takes the second step of assured discipleship. Faith is the root; assurance is the flower.

Faith is the trembling woman who reached out to touch the hem of the garment of Christ. Assurance is Job sitting in an ash pile, broken out with boils and saying, "Though he slay me, yet will I trust in him . . ." (Job 13:15 KJV).

Faith is the penitent thief hanging on a cross, crying out, ". . . Jesus, remember me when you come into your kingdom" (Luke 23:42 NIV). Assurance is Stephen dying for his faith with the testimony ". . . I see heaven open and the Son of Man standing at the right hand of God" (Acts 7:56 NIV).

Faith is Saul of Tarsus on the road to Damascus, "Who are you, Lord? . . ." (Acts 9:5 NIV.) Assurance is Paul the apostle in the Roman prison, "I have fought the good fight, I have finished the race, I have kept the faith" (2 Timothy 4:7 NIV).

Faith is Peter the fisherman trying to walk on the water, ". . . Lord, save me!" (Matthew 14:30 NIV). Assurance is Peter the apostle on the day of Pentecost, ". . . Repent and be baptized . . . . And you will receive the gift of the Holy Spirit" (Acts 2:38 NIV).

Actualize your calling! Move from fractured feelings to a functional faith.

John, a young college student in Georgia, did this. He grew up in a wealthy home and had every opportunity to gain fame and fortune. Upon graduation from college, his father gave him a trip around the world. After returning, he was impressed to go back to Brazil as a missionary to poverty-stricken Indians. Over the protests of his family and the dismay of his friends, John served as a missionary and served well. While ministering in the jungles, he succumbed to a severe illness and subsequently died because of improper medical care. At the close of his funeral here in the United States, one of his friends was heard to remark,

"It is a pity. John could have had everything, yet he died with nothing." Another friend, hearing the remark, replied, "Perhaps! But when you really analyze it, John had everything and died for something because he gave his life in service to others."

We all won't do it just like this young man, but we all have a personal calling to fulfill. The way we affirm this calling, make the most of our opportunities, and accent our faith will make the difference. Like the disciples, we can move from fractured feelings to a functional faith.

5

You Can Win With Worry

What is the most frightening experience you have ever had? A sudden accident? A devastating sickness? A near tragedy? The ravages of combat in war? The terrifying experience of being lost or left alone?

Whatever the answer, most of us have had a frightening experience in a storm, for storms are very much a part of our lives. Every year some ten hurricanes sweep across our country and leave a wake of destruction and devastation. Sometimes we call them cyclones or typhoons; but, regardless of the terminology, hurricanes mean winds up to two hundred miles per hour. It is these winds which have caused approximately fifteen hundred deaths and 20 billion dollars in property damage over the past twenty years.

Then there are tornadoes. Between five hundred and six hundred of them rip across the countryside every year. While there are no instruments capable of direct measurement of their wind velocity, indirect measurement shows winds over two hundred and fifty miles per hour, with a force that can drive a broom straw through a two-by-four piece of lumber.

We all know about meteorological storms, but what about the emotional storm of worry? Like the disciples in Matthew 8, we have all experienced what they must have felt when, suddenly, "Without warning, a furious storm came up on the lake, so that the waves swept over the boat. But Jesus was sleeping. The disciples went and woke him, saying, 'Lord, save us! We're going to drown!' " (Matthew 8:24, 25 NIV).

To understand this story, we have to get the setting and take a look at the Sea of Galilee. It is just a small lake, eight miles wide and fourteen miles long. The problem is that it is situated where the Jordan Valley makes a cleft in the very rim of the earth, creating a depth of approximately six hundred and eighty feet below sea level. It is bordered on the east side by the Golan Heights, comprised of limestone rock standing two thousand feet above the sea and merging into the Gilead Mountains. It is bordered on the west side by valleys, hills, crevasses, and rocks. The result is a natural funnel which draws winds from the west side through the cracks and crevasses into powerful air swirls which hit the sea with a glancing blow, bounce off the Golan Heights, and return to the sea, causing a whiplash motion and creating high, variable turbulence with tall, devastating waves.

Thus, the Sea of Galilee is a geological deception. On the one hand, it is very calm, serene, tranquil, and gracious. On the other hand, it can be lashed into a storm of earthquake proportions, with winds coming from every direction and waves so high that the boats are hidden from view.

In many respects, this is what happens in our own lives. Winds come from every direction. Waves get so high we get lost from view, and, just like the disciples, we panic. We cry out to God, "Don't You care about us? The waves are in the boat! The ship is about to be swamped! We are going to drown, and You are asleep!"

The pressure of life hits us, and we get worried. But what is this thing called worry? What really happens when we get this way?

For starters, worry is fear, and fear does strange things to us. It immobilizes us, makes us uptight, and causes extreme anxiety. Our muscles become tense. Our breathing gets deeper and faster. Our heartbeat rates increase rapidly. Our blood vessels constrict; our blood pressure rises; our perspiration increases. The pituitary glands and adrenal glands begin to pump hormones into our bodies, and our systems become alarm reactors. As a result, we sometimes get a giddy feeling, to the point where we feel detached from the situation and wonder if what's going on is really happening to us.

Worry is a sense of prolonged stress to the point of distraction. It is a state of the mind and a condition of the emotions. We feel helpless and hapless. We feel incapable and inadequate. We feel harassed, tormented, and plagued. It is an incessant kind of frustration that causes us to become despondent, depressed, and inactive. We don't know what decisions to make. We are not sure what alternatives to choose. We just don't have the right answers, and we really are not sure of the right questions.

Yet here we are in the twentieth century, living in the most affluent society ever devised; so why are we so worried? What is it that keeps us uptight?

For one thing, we worry about the threat of international disaster. Will there be enough food to feed the world? Will there be clean air to breathe? Will there be pure water to drink? Will somebody push the mythical "end of time" button and throw the world into atomic oblivion?

We worry about our national situation: our politics, the economy, our morality, the crime rate, rising inflation, and our future as a nation. Can democracy survive? Can the Republic really last? Will the Constitution really see us through? Do we have the leadership we need, or has the American dream turned into a nightmare?

Most of the time it gets more personal. The waves get in the boat, and we battle an individual storm. When we don't have a job, it's a storm. When we can't pay our bills, it's a storm. When we are heavily in debt, it's a storm. When we are on the verge of a divorce, it's a storm. When we feel as if we have lost touch with our children, it's a storm.

The end result is that we feel as if we are in a deep, dark pit where light cannot penetrate. We become restless, nervous, and filled with dread. We dread to think of the future. We dread sickness, old age, dependency, and death. We dread facing a job that we don't really like. We dread coming home at night because of a tension-filled house and the hostility of unresolved conflicts. It all eats away at us, and we call it worry.

Then when it looks like the end, Christ steps up and in one statement—"Peace, be still!"—the whole scene changes. The wind dies down. It becomes completely calm, and He says to His disciples, ". . . Why are you so afraid? Have you still no faith?" (Mark 4:40 NIV).

Suddenly, we know that in Christ we can win with worry. In fact, the apostle Paul tells us in no uncertain terms, "Don't worry over anything whatever . . ." (Philippians 4:6 PHILLIPS). Then he goes on to chart the course by saying:

> . . . tell God every detail of your needs in earnest and thankful prayer, and the peace of God, which transcends human understanding, will keep constant guard over your hearts and minds as they rest in Christ Jesus. Here is a last piece of advice. If you believe in goodness and if you value the approval of God, fix your minds on the things which are holy and right and pure and beautiful and good.
>
> Philippians 4:6–8 PHILLIPS

In short, here is a plan to win with worry!

Pray in Detail

". . . tell God every detail of your needs in earnest and thankful prayer . . ." (Philippians 4:6 PHILLIPS). This is the beginning point—learn to pray in a way that will bring results. Tell God the details of your needs in an attitude of thankfulness.

God has promised to answer. In the Old Testament, the prophet Isaiah tells us, "Then, if you call, the Lord will answer; if you cry to him, he will say, 'Here I am.' If you cease to pervert justice, to point the accusing finger and lay false charges" (Isaiah 58:9 NEB).

In the New Testament, Christ promises us that if we ask, it will be given; if we seek, we will find; if we knock, it will be opened. "For everyone who asks receives; he who seeks finds; and to him who knocks, the door will be opened" (Luke 11:10 NIV).

Will it work here in the twentieth century? In answer, here is a letter received from a woman in Durban, South Africa:

> This letter should have been written months ago. Please forgive me for that! I received a wonderful healing through listening to the Mount Paran Worship Hour. It was the Thursday evening before Easter . . . the Spirit of God was so near. In the service you said, "Jesus is here to heal you." I had a hard growth in my right ear for over a year and knew only surgery, of which I was terrified, could remove it. However, as I felt the presence of the Lord to be so real, I placed my finger to my ear and said, "Please, Jesus, touch my ear." I have to be honest when I say this, that I never believed I would experience a miracle.
>
> Good Friday and Saturday passed, and I never thought anymore about it. On Sunday morning I was preparing for church when I put my finger in my ear and felt no growth there. I was trembling with excitement and called my husband to have a look.
>
> He was astounded. It had disappeared completely, and not a scar was left. Oh, how I praise God for this miracle. I feel so unworthy of such love. It disappeared with no sign of pain or even an itch or bleeding. Isn't the Lord wonderful? I have witnessed to all about my healing . . . .

This is the way to win with worry. ". . . tell God every detail of your needs in earnest and thankful prayer . . ." (Philippians 4:6 PHILLIPS).

Practice the Peace of God

Following the affirmation of prayer, Paul gives us the second phase of the plan by stating: ". . . the peace of God, which transcends human understanding, will keep constant guard over your hearts and minds as they rest in Christ Jesus" (Philippians 4:7 PHILLIPS).

Of all the statements in the Bible, this is perhaps the most profound. Think of it! The peace of God stands as a guard over our hearts and minds. We can actually rest in Christ Jesus without worry or fear.

This is the legacy Christ has left us. Christ states, "Peace I leave with you, my peace I give unto you: not as the world giveth, give I unto you. Let not your heart be troubled, neither let it be afraid" (John 14:27 KJV). In John 16:33 He makes us this promise, "These things I have spoken unto you, that in me ye might have peace. In the world ye shall have tribulation: but be of good cheer; I have overcome the world" (KJV).

The question is, "How do we get to that? How do we learn to practice peace?" The answer is found in releasing the potential power we each have to appropriate the very glory of God into our own lives, regardless of the circumstances. Second Corinthians 3:18 tells us that ". . . [we] reflect like mirrors the glory of the Lord . . ." (PHILLIPS). This really means that we reflect the character of God, the magnificence of God, the righteousness of God, the excellence of God, the grace and dignity of God. Isaiah states that:

He gives vigour to the weary, new strength to the exhausted. Young men may grow weary and faint, even in their prime they may stumble and fall; but

those who look to the Lord will win new strength, they
will grow wings like eagles; they will run and not be
weary, they will march on and never grow faint.
Isaiah 40:29–31 NEB

The point is that each one of us has the potentiality of the
spirit of an eagle. We can have this sense of freedom. In
God's peace we can defeat worry at every turn.

I was once preparing a sermon on this Isaiah text and
asked my wife, Carmelita, what she knew about eagles. She
answered, "Not much, but I'll do some research for you." I
thought she would come up with the usual facts about
wingspan, habits, and flying ability, but instead she said, "I
have found out eight things about an eagle: He soars high.
He flies fast. He sees far. He lives long. He hides well. He
has extreme confidence. He has clean habits, and he looks
after his family."

This is the spirit of practicing peace, and this is the power
that overcomes worry. God wants each one of us to soar
high, fly fast, see far, live long, hide well, exert extreme
confidence, practice clean habits, and look after our
families. With His Spirit motivating this process, we can
always win with worry.

Program Your Thinking

Finally, Paul brings the entire plan into focus with the
statement ". . . fix your minds on the things which are holy
and right and pure and beautiful and good" (Philippians 4:8
PHILLIPS).

The apostle knew that we would be confronting a brain-
washed world. He was aware of a coming pressure-cooker
age, designed to stretch us to the breaking point, until we
would lose our sense of objectivity, our sense of absolutes,
our sense of divine identity, and our sense of spiritual values. That is why he calls for a positive mind set in this text
and a renewed mind in Romans 12:2.

You see, the brain is the most complex mechanism ever created. In one way it is like a telephone switchboard that connects incoming and outgoing calls. In another way it is like a computer that makes decisions about which circuits to link and which calls to connect. However, the crowning achievement of the brain is the capacity to think, perceive, and experience. Further, the way in which these three processes combine determines what we call learning. In turn, what we learn and how we evaluate this new information shapes our behavior and the kind of life-style we pursue.

In a very real sense, we are what we think. Proverbs 23:7 says that as we think in our hearts, so we are. Paul says that we need to be transformed by the renewing of our minds (*see* Romans 12:2).

To be transformed is to change form completely, as illustrated in the transfiguration of Christ (*see* Matthew 17) or the transition of a caterpillar to a butterfly. It is to undergo a spiritual metamorphosis. To be renewed is to experience a thinking renovation with a subsequent change in character toward the excellency of Christ. It is to program our brains with the power of Christ to the point where we can truly fix our minds on ". . . the things which are holy and right and pure and beautiful and good" (Philippians 4:8 PHILLIPS).

Perhaps it is best illustrated by a letter from a seventeen-year-old in South Africa:

I quite by mistake managed to pick up your church's broadcast on the twenty-fourth of July. I'm seventeen years old, and I've recently accepted Christ as Saviour, after having run from Him for over four years. During this time I tried to shut God out of my life by turning to drugs, spiritualism, and suicide. I have tried suicide three times, only to be discovered just in time. I was extremely rebellious in a quiet, bitter, and resentful way. I refused to make friendships because I saw no good in myself, and I didn't want others to see how bad

I was, too. I literally hated myself through and through. Eventually I came to a point where I realized, "Man, if I don't stop and rethink and reevaluate my life, I am in big trouble." Praise the Lord! I heard the gospel and realized how filthy I was in God's sight. I asked for forgiveness, and now I'M FREE! Oh, I've had hassles. It's not easy just to give up drugs and spiritualism and expect no troubles. I think I've learned the hard way. Now Christ guides my life and gives me reason for living and a life of joy and happiness—not a life of hate and bitterness.

"Man, if I don't stop and rethink and reevaluate my life, I am in big trouble!" This is the process. Program your thinking. This is the plan that turned this girl's life around.

This is the plan that will win with worry. Pray in detail. Practice the peace of God. Program your thinking. It will work! The Bible is true! "Don't worry over anything whatever . . ." (Philippians 4:6 PHILLIPS).

6

You Can Defuse Depression

If I were to ask you, "What is the number-one illness in the United States?" what would you answer? Many of us would probably say cancer, heart disease, arthritis, leukemia, emphysema, or some other illness with which we are acquainted.

The truth is that the number-one illness in our country today is an emotional illness—an illness that we call depression. Because of depression one hundred twenty-five thousand people are hospitalized each year. Because of depression an additional two hundred thousand or more seek psychiatric help, and approximately seventy thousand people annually commit suicide.

If we are honest, none of us are exempt. We all experience depression to some degree and can probably identify with Job when he says,

So months of futility are my portion, troubled nights are my lot. When I lie down, I think, "When will it be day that I may rise?" . . . I do nothing but toss till morning twilight. My body is infested with worms, and scabs cover my skin. My days are swifter than a shuttle and come to an end as the thread runs out.

Job 7:3–6 NEB

Any way we look at it, this expression of Job's is about as sad a picture as we can describe. In our terms, Job is saying, "I've had it! I'm down to the end! I can't sleep. I can't

61

eat. I'm broken out with a terrible rash and feel as if I'm going to die any minute." In short, Job was depressed.

We've all been there and sometimes feel like the man who sat in my office and exclaimed, "I just flew in from out of state in my private jet. I make over one hundred thousand dollars per year. I can buy anything I want, but tell me, Dr. Walker, why am I always so depressed?"

It's an important question, and in answer some might say, "Let me try your one-hundred-thousand-dollar-a-year life-style, and maybe I can tell a little better why you're depressed."

One hundred thousand dollars a year or not, depression puts us down and makes us feel so low that we think we have to reach up to touch bottom. In fact, it may be like the automobile mechanic who went to a psychiatrist. The psychiatrist said, "Tell me, sir, what is your occupation?" He said, "I'm an automobile mechanic." To which the psychiatrist replied, "Well, in that case, lie down here *under* the couch." Sometimes we feel the same way—under the pile of our problems.

Then we back off and say, "What do we really mean when we talk about depression? What is it? How is it defined?"

In a word, it is a strange kind of gloom that seems to settle down upon us. It threatens our life-styles and changes our moods. It affects the kind of persons we are and the degree of happiness or unhappiness we experience. We call it by many different names—melancholia, lethargy, withdrawal—but it all boils down to the same thing. Our spirits are down!

Psychologically there are no easy answers for the cause of depression. Some people say it is aggression turned inward. We become angry and turn it on ourselves. Others say it is the result of separation and alienation. We become separated from our resources. We feel useless and inadequate. We run out of options and can see no way out.

At any rate, we get caught in a syndrome of self-criticism, self-doubt, and self-pity. We suffer from loss of appetite, sleeplessness, and could care less about our appearances. We experience sorrow, distress, and irritability. We withdraw, become apathetic, and, in the most severe instances, become catatonic. Spiritually we are prone to question God, discount His will, reject His word, and refuse to utilize His resources.

A tragic picture, to be sure; so what do we do about it? What do we do when we get to the end of our ropes and don't know where to turn?

This is when the Bible speaks the loudest. This is when the resources of the Lord become the most important. This is when the power of Jesus Christ has the greatest message for us. The Bible tells us that we can defuse depression. We can deactivate it. We can detonate it. We can take the sting out of it. We can take the explosion out of it. We can take the control out of it.

Sounds great, doesn't it? The question is *how?*

In answer, let's take a look at the life of an Old Testament prophet named Elijah. We don't know much about his background; we only know that he was a Tishbite, but no one seems to know for sure just who the Tishbites were. We do know that Elijah came from the rugged mountains of Gilead. We do know that he was accustomed to the rough and savage life-style of a herdsman and mountaineer. We do know that the hot Syrian sun had bronzed his brow, and its red-hot heat had pierced his eyes so that he was a man to look at and tremble.

Above all we know that Elijah was a man of God who dared to stand up to the wickedness of King Ahab and Queen Jezebel. Elijah was the kind of man who "called a spade a spade" and thus would denounce the idolatry of a king and queen who had substituted baalism, a vile, cruel, heathenistic religion, for the worship of the one true God. Elijah had, by the power of God, brought about a drought that lasted three and one-half years. Because of his faith, he was able to provide the widow of Zarephath with a cruse of oil and a jar of flour that never diminished. Because of his faith, God raised the widow's son from the dead. Through Elijah, God sent down fire from heaven and destroyed four hundred prophets of Baal. Later, the Lord gave him special strength so that he was able to run seventeen miles ahead of Ahab's chariot to the entrance of the city of Jezreel.

Yet with all that power and all those miracles, we also know that Elijah was a man. In fact, the apostle James tells us, "Elijah was a man just like us . . ." (James 5:17 NIV). Consequently, we find him in 1 Kings 19:4 sitting under a juniper tree and praying to die. The elation of his spiritual and physical victories had passed, and the accompanying strain had left him in the grip of depression, fear, and disappointment. Jezebel was threatening his life, and he felt desperately alone. "I've had enough," he told the Lord. "Take away my life. I've got to die sometime, and it might as well be now."

Here he is, Elijah—God's great hero—sniveling like a little child and suffering the throes of depression. On the flip side, however, Elijah didn't stay in that condition. He moved out from the bush. He defused his depression.

How did he do it? That is the question!

Notice the dialogue between God and Elijah, and the process becomes apparent.

Life Moves in Cycles

First, God sent angels to minister to Elijah, and we read a profound statement that is often overlooked, ". . . Arise and eat; because the journey is too great for thee" (1 Kings 19:7 KJV).

In other words, recognize that life moves in cycles. It has its ups and downs. It arranges itself in peaks and valleys. Some days we're on the top; other days we're on the bottom. The point is that normal living, with all of its pressure, problems, and hectic pace takes its toll and leaves us with the blues. To be down does not mean that we are abandoned by God. To be down does not mean we do not have faith. To be down does not mean we have lost a Christian witness. To be always euphoric or ecstatic may mean we are hiding from ourselves and playing a very destructive game that eventually can erode our minds and turn into mental disorder. The point is that life is normal when it moves in cycles.

Function, Whether You Feel Like It or Not

The second step in the process is that God told Elijah, ". . . Go forth and stand upon the mount before the Lord . . ." (v. 11 KJV). In other words, function, whether you feel like it or not. No one says we have to quit living because we feel depressed. The dishes have to be washed; the shirts have to be ironed; the office has to be run; the deal has to be closed; life goes on, regardless of how we feel.

In effect, God told Elijah, "Function, whether you feel like it or not. It doesn't matter that you're cold, muddy, depressed, and discouraged. Get up! Quit feeling sorry for yourself and stand on the mountain before the Lord!"

The best time to worship is when we're depressed. The best time to pray is when we're depressed. The best time to sing is when we're depressed. It is extremely difficult to stay depressed when we really worship God in prayer and praise. Paul and Silas found this out in the Philippian jail, and at midnight, after being rudely apprehended, publicly ridiculed, mercilessly beaten, illegally thrown in prison, and painfully locked in stocks, ". . . Paul and Silas were praying and singing hymns to God . . ." (Acts 16:25 NIV).

Remember the outcome! "Suddenly there was such a violent earthquake that the foundations of the prison were shaken. At once all the prison doors flew open, and everybody's chains came loose" (Acts 16:26 NIV). Ultimately Paul and Silas were not only released but officially escorted from the prison (*see* Acts 16:26–40) and the message is, "Function, whether you feel like it or not!"

Touch Your Assurance Point

Thus, Elijah went up to the mountain, and as he stood there, wondering what to do next, the Bible tells us that:

> . . . For the Lord was passing by: a great and strong wind came rending mountains and shattering rocks before him, but the Lord was not in the wind; and after the wind there was an earthquake, but the Lord was not in the earthquake; and after the earthquake fire, but the Lord was not in the fire; and after the fire a low murmuring sound.
>
> 1 Kings 19:11–13 NEB

The King James Version translates it a "still small voice." Elijah got in touch with his assurance point of faith. He communed with the heart of God.

Here was a man bent all out of shape. As far as he was concerned, he was the only faithful person left. In his view, the people of Israel had forsaken God's covenant, torn down His altars, and put His prophets to death with the sword. In his words, ". . . I alone am left, and they seek to take my life" (1 Kings 19:14 NEB), but Elijah heard from God. He touched his assurance point, and the Lord revealed to him that there were seven thousand in Israel who had neither bowed to Baal nor kissed him (*see* 1 Kings 19:18).

Too often we look for God in the earthquake and fire and fail to hear the still small voice. That is why the third step in defusing depression is to touch the assurance point. This is the whole point of Christ's coming into the world—to give us a sense of confidence and assurance, regardless of the circumstances. Christ came to free us from depression.

That is why the Bible talks about a life of peace (*see*

Romans 5:1), a life of transformation (*see* 2 Corinthians 5:17), a life of joy (*see* John 16:24), a life of purpose (*see* Matthew 6:33), a life of confidence (*see* 1 John 5:14, 15), and a life of full pardon (*see* 1 John 1:9). To suffer temporary depression is normal. To stay depressed is to deny ourselves God's resources in Christ.

How can we stay depressed if we live a life of peace? How can we stay depressed if we live a life of transformation? How can we stay depressed if we live a life of joy, purpose, and confidence? How can we stay depressed if we live a life of full pardon from sin?

This is the assurance point! ". . . Everything is possible for him who believes" (Mark 9:23 NIV).

Susan found this out, and in the following letter gives a vivid account of her personal search:

    . . . about five years ago, I thought I was really living. I was popular with the men, and my ego really got a boost. I have always had a very poor self-image, and I guess I reinforced it with bad behavior . . . . I thought I was really living, but deep down it was slowly catching up with me.

    I know I was going against my true philosophy in life, but I didn't know it until *depression* set in. A lot of things happened that shouldn't have happened, and my husband and I learned to hate each other . . . .

    I began to withdraw. I didn't want to go out or see anybody . . . . I hated myself . . . . I ended up sitting in a chair in the living room, staring into space, unable to function. I barely managed to take care of the minimal needs of my children, and I even wished that my husband were dead . . . . This led to more guilt and depression. Finally I reached the point of considering suicide. I was fixing myself a "Black Russian" or two, sometimes three, by 5:00 P.M. every day . . . .

    Then, through a friend, I was led to a Christian counseling center and eventually to your church. In the process my husband and I met the Lord and found Jesus Christ.

I can't begin to tell you all the areas that God has cleaned up in my life. I had a foul mouth, and I could have put any truck driver to shame. I had a terrible time with alcohol until I turned it over to God, and He really scrubbed me out. I was smoking nearly three packs of cigarettes a day, and He carried me through cold-turkey quitting.

I yelled and screamed at my children all the time. He was gracious enough to help me learn kindness and mercy, and then, to beat it all, the kids can't recall how mean I used to be. He has given me a love for all people, and a responsiveness and sensitivity that has enabled me to minister His love to some of the people with whom I had real problems.

Oh, I still have a long way to go, but at least I am going in the right direction now. When I trip, Jesus is there to reach down and give me a hand and set me back on my feet again. I have felt His touch many times, and there is nothing in this world to take His place.

Booze? Who needs it? . . . I can find greater blessings in Christ . . . . And I can say now, after fifteen years of marriage and trying it both ways . . . the only way is with Jesus.

Get Outside of Yourself

Finally, God told Elijah one last thing. Get outside of yourself. Do something for somebody else. "The Lord said to him, 'Go back by way of the wilderness of Damascus, enter the city and anoint Hazael to be king of Aram; anoint Jehu . . . to be king of Israel, and Elisha . . . to be prophet in your place' " (1 Kings 19:15–17 NEB).

You see, the essential element in depression is becoming

ingrown and locked into our own lives. We can see only ourselves and our own plights. Consequently we lose our usefulness and our sense of being needed and wanted.

This happened to Elijah, but God sent him out to do His work and fulfill his office as a prophet.

Perhaps it is best expressed by an experience of a pastor who was interviewing prospective new members for his church. He had been forewarned that one woman who would seek membership had created problems in several other churches in the city. She was bitter and depressed because of a severe back injury she had suffered as a child. It had disfigured her body and warped her personality. She gained attention by aggressive and disruptive actions which had caused great dissension in other church fellowships.

Being aware of the situation, the pastor called her aside and said, "Before you can become a member of this church, I want to talk to you." Later, in his office, he told her, "Look, you've got a reputation, and we don't need your kind of spirit in this church. We want you here if this is where you think God wants you, but before you join there is an assignment you will have to fulfill. Every Monday morning I want you to come to this church and pick up a list of people who are sick, shut-in and hospitalized. I want you to visit at least five of these every week for six months. After you have done this I will talk to you again about joining this church."

Obviously it startled the woman. No one had ever talked to her like that, but she decided to do it. She had sufficient personal support from an inheritance, which meant she had no job and really had too much time to translate her handicaps into resentment and hate.

Every Monday she picked up the names without fail. It was difficult for her at first. She was blocked by bitterness and hostility, to the point that it was very awkward to relate to the hurt and suffering of others. However, little by little she started giving of herself to people in much worse conditions than she. Week by week a miracle grew in her life, until she became one of the most radiant people in that congregation and fulfilled a most meaningful ministry to others. Thus, when she entered into membership, she came bringing a new life and a dimension of service which challenged the entire congregation.

There is no doubt about it! Depression can be an insidious emotional disease, but we have the resources in Christ to defuse its power and control its influence. Elijah did it, and here is his formula:

Recognize that life moves in cycles.
Function, whether you feel like it or not.
Touch your assurance point.
Get outside of yourself.

7

From Handicaps to Handles

Thomas Carlyle once made the statement that for every person who can handle prosperity there are a hundred who can handle adversity. As strange as this statement may be, the way we handle adversity says much about whether or not we ever achieve prosperity.

Adversity has a way of bringing out the best in us. Prosperity has a way of tranquilizing us. Adversity has a way of pushing us to utilize all available resources. Prosperity has a way of romanticizing our own abilities and stymieing our continued development. Adversity has a way of putting life in true perspective and forcing us to face reality. Prosperity opens the door for inordinate pride and conceited fantasy.

Sometimes we find ourselves in the position of Israel. In the wilderness, Israel was a nation composed of resolute, determined, committed people with a purpose in mind and a goal to achieve. Then they reached the Promised Land. Suddenly all their needs were met. All the necessities of life were available to them. They had curds from the herds. They had milk from the flocks. They had fat from the lambs and the rams. They had meat from the herds of Bashan. They had wheat from the fields. They had wine from the blood of the grape.

What happened? Israel waxed fat and kicked. Israel forsook God and turned her back on the source of salvation. Israel married strange wives, worshiped heathen gods, and forgot the commandments of the Lord.

What was the result? Israel was scattered abroad and

spent a millennium trying to find her meaning and restore her identity. As an old Italian proverb once said, "In times of prosperity no altars smoke."

Isn't this our problem today? We find ourselves at the altars, and the fires have gone out. Even the fire in our national heart has grown dim: We bow to the gods of reason; we worship the gods of work; we are preoccupied by the gods of sex; we pursue the gods of violent entertainment and march toward destruction to the tunes of the gods of the flesh.

Now we're faced with adversity, and we're not quite sure how to handle it. The international control of wealth has shifted. Military superiority has changed hands. We're no longer sure we're the most powerful or greatest nation in the world. Suddenly the giant is sick, and there is no quick cure.

Handicaps

So how do we handle adversity? We face it at every level, and it hits us, each one, in a different way.

For instance, a baby is born, contracts poliomyelitis, and grows up a cripple. One day he realizes he can't run and play like the others. He can't compete on the same level, and he lives with a physical handicap.

Here is a woman who looks inside herself and knows there is something desperately wrong. As a child she was abused and neglected. Now she reaps the pain of ingrained habits and conditioned behavior patterns that cause fear, bitterness, hate, and anger. She battles a seething rage that shortchanges her relationships. She lives with an emotional handicap.

Then what about the young man who had all his dreams ahead of him. He had made such plans. He was going to achieve such greatness, but every time he pressed on the accelerator, there just wasn't enough power. He never quite made it. One day in his forties he had to face the fact that he would never compose the music, never paint the pictures, never build the skyscraper, never own his business, and never be the president of the company. He lives with an intellectual handicap.

It's true! Each one of us has experienced it. Some of us are going through it right now. Something inside us goes limp. Something inside us dies. We feel caught and desperately need some handles.

But how do we turn handicaps into handles? Where is the prescription? What is the formula?

The apostle Paul learned how the hard way, and we hear him say, "We are handicapped on all sides but we are never frustrated: we are puzzled, but never in despair. We are persecuted, but we never have to stand it alone: we may be knocked down but we are never knocked out!" (2 Corinthians 4:8, 9 PHILLIPS.)

Then we say, "It sounds too easy. Just saying it doesn't make it so." And it's true—sometimes we want easy answers, quick solutions, and instantaneous changes without personal commitment, emotional growth, and responsible action.

We get caught in the do-it-yourself-quick syndrome, which brings to mind the classic story of the Catholic and Jewish couples who lived side by side in a duplex. For the Catholics every Friday was "fish only," but for the Jews it was barbecue-steak-in-the-backyard night. To eat fish to the aroma of barbecued steak Friday after Friday was more than the Catholic couple could bear. Finally, after much deliberation, the only solution seemed to be to convert the Jewish couple to Catholicism and thus have them join the fish-on-Friday ritual. After several weeks their objective was reached, and with joy they watched the holy water sprinkled and heard the words of the officiant, "You were born a Hebrew, raised a Jew, but I baptize you a Catholic." What a victory! What a relief! No more smell of barbecued steak on Friday.

The next Friday rolled around. To the Catholic couple's dismay, the same aroma of barbecued steak came drifting through the apartment from the backyard. Horrified, they ran out to see what could have brought about such sudden backsliding. To their surprise, the Jewish husband was standing over a simmering steak on the outdoor grill, sprinkling it with barbecue sauce and saying in solemn tones, "You were born a calf, raised a cow, and I baptize you a fish."

Obviously, it just doesn't work that way! But the question is *how?* How do we turn our handicaps into handles?

Handles

Here is where the Bible makes its most important contribution; it never leaves us without methods and means. Thus we hear the same apostle Paul say:

> This is the reason why we never collapse. The outward man does indeed suffer wear and tear, but every day the inward man receives fresh strength. These little troubles (which are really so transitory) are winning for us a permanent and glorious reward out of all proportion to our pain.
>
> 2 Corinthians 4:16, 17 PHILLIPS

For starters these Scriptures give us three principles of living that will bring results.

Principle 1: We turn our handicaps into handles when we research our resources. Paul saw some resources to keep us from collapsing, and he labeled them as eternal; thus we join him in saying:

> We want our transitory life to be absorbed into the Life that is eternal. Now the power that has planned this experience for us is God, and He has given us His Spirit as a guarantee of its truth. This makes us confident, whatever happens.
>
> 2 Corinthians 5:4, 5 PHILLIPS

"This makes us confident, whatever happens"? Will that really work? It worked for John Milton, and out of his blindness came *Paradise Lost* and *Paradise Regained*. It worked for Ludwig van Beethoven, and out of his deafness came the Ninth Symphony. It worked for John Bunyan, and out of his imprisonment came *Pilgrim's Progress*. It worked for Helen Keller, and out of her deafness and blindness came an inner power that could exclaim, ". . . neither darkness nor silence can impede the progress of the human spirit."

The point is that each one of these people turned their handicaps into handles. They researched their resources, turned what they had to use over to the power of God, and emerged with giant contributions to humanity as a whole. And the beauty of it is that we can do the same.

For instance, a man sat in my office and in a matter-of-fact voice said, "I made three bad decisions last year, and it cost me ten million dollars. In fact, this year has been the year of a new start, because I have had to begin from scratch." Well, to hear such staggering losses talked about in such matter-of-fact terms boggled my mind, particularly when it is a major task for me to keep my checkbook balanced, let alone talk about losing ten million dollars.

So I asked him, "How can you be so matter-of-fact? How can you be so calm about it all?" In answer, he said, "You should have seen me a month ago. I was in a deep depression and on the verge of suicide. I had built an empire, and in one year it crashed to the ground all around my head. Finally, in desperation, I cried out to God just to take my life and save my family further embarrassment by the stigma of my suicide." Then he said, "Do you know what God put in my heart? 'Why are you so upset? You still have everything that really counts. Why don't you count your blessings, turn them over to Me, and I will show you a better life.' That was the turning point! I did just that. I still had my family, my health, a heavily mortgaged house, and the prospect of a job. Most important of all, I still had my faith. So I went out and went after it. I still have some 'downers,' but in the process I am discovering new re- sources of faith. I am living a much happier, though less grandiose, life-style than I have ever known. For me it is a matter of researching my resources and letting God help me put them to work."

"This is the reason why we never collapse": We have eternal resources.

Principle 2: We turn our handicaps into handles when we retune our responses to life. Paul puts this concept in perspective by saying, "The outward man does indeed suf- fer wear and tear, but every day the inward man receives fresh strength" (2 Corinthians 4:16 PHILLIPS). The truth is that we are constantly having to tune and retune the way we react to life. On the one hand, we can live extrinsically and be pushed around from the outside by all our daily troubles; or on the other hand, we can opt to live intrinsically and govern our lives from the inside, with a constant retuning to the power of God within us.

Demas lived from the outside. He apparently left the faith because he loved the world (*see* 2 Timothy 4:10). Paul lived from the inside and learned ". . . to be content whatever the circumstances" (Philippians 4:11 NIV). Demas evidently structured his life by temporary values, while Paul struc- tured his life by eternal values which transcend the daily pressures. For this reason he could say, "These little trou- bles (which are really so transitory) are winning for us a permanent and glorious reward out of all proportion to our pain" (2 Corinthians 4:17 PHILLIPS).

The point is that we have the capacities to become bigger than our situations. We are not made out of wood, hay, and stubble that burns. We are not made out of metal that can be melted away. We are made out of eternal stuff; we are very valuable in God's sight; we are made to last forever. It's all a matter of tuning.

George Matheson, the great hymn writer, found this out. As a young man, he lost his eyesight in an accident; how-

ever, on the spot he made a decision to retune his responses
to life. Matheson made himself the vow "I will reach every
goal I have set—blindness or not." A look at his life bears it
out. He retuned and became bigger than life. Now, every
Lord's Day, somewhere people worship and sing the hymn
of his heart:

> O Love that wilt not let me go,
> I rest my weary soul in Thee;
> I give Thee back the life I owe,
> That in Thine ocean depths its flow
> May richer, fuller be.

*Principle 3: We turn our handicaps into handles when we
reorder our priorities.* In this regard Paul tells us that we
have to look all the time ". . . not at the visible things but
at the invisible. The visible things are transitory; it is the
invisible things that are really permanent" (2 Corinthians
4:18 PHILLIPS).

Christ also saw the importance of this principle and made
the statement that ". . . where your treasure is, there your
heart will be also" (Matthew 6:21 NIV).

What all this really means is that handles are a matter of
priorities. We have the option of living by the secular
priorities that place importance on the visible things, or the
spiritual priorities that emphasize the invisible things.

On the secular side, we are caught up in the *me* syndrome, in which we have moved to a compulsive taking
care of ourselves. It's as though we are in a revival of
narcissism, in which we want to live for the big *I*. Consequently, we have fathers who don't want to father,
mothers who don't want to mother, children who don't
want responsibilities, and a life-style that is void of joy,
hope, meaning, and faith.

Like Narcissus, we sit and look at our distorted images in
the pool. In the name of humanism we have made God the
symbol of our own powers and defined faith in terms of the

certainty of our own convictions, based on our own experiences of thought and feeling.

On the spiritual side, there is another option—making the invisible things really permanent. To do this, we set up our life-styles by faith in God and view life from a transcendental self in the process of developing in the image of Christ. In this model ". . . all of us who are Christians have no veils on our faces, but reflect like mirrors the glory of the Lord. We are transfigured by the Spirit of the Lord in ever-increasing splendour into His own image" (2 Corinthians 3:18 PHILLIPS).

This means that when the chips are down and the handicaps have us trapped, we have a resource of spiritual strength. We have the power ". . . to live by trusting Him without seeing Him" (2 Corinthians 5:7 PHILLIPS). To use the words of Paul, "We are so sure of this that we would really rather be 'away' from the body and be 'at home' with the Lord. It is our aim therefore, to please Him . . ." (2 Corinthians 5:8, 9 PHILLIPS).

This kind of spirit is the strength of our faith, and it is fully reflected in the testimony of an early church Christian martyr who turned his handicaps into handles through the power of spiritual priorities. Here is what he writes from a deep, dark dungeon:

> In a dark hole I have found cheerfulness; in a place of bitterness and death I have found rest. While others weep I have found laughter, where others fear I have found strength. Who would believe that in a state of misery I have had great pleasure; that in a lonely corner I have glorious company, and in the hardest bonds perfect repose. All these things Jesus has granted me. He is with me, comforts me and fills me with joy. He drives bitterness from me and fills me with strength and consolation.

"This is the reason why we never collapse." In Christ we have the power to move from handicaps to handles.

8

Which Way Is Up?

The fog was so thick you could have cut it with a knife. The pilot of the small Piper Cub broke out in a cold sweat. Suddenly he realized that he was enmeshed in an enveloping and smothering cloud bank. Visibility was zero. His sense of direction was confused.

Without warning, the plane went into a spin and began to plummet toward the ground through an open space in the clouds. The operator in the control tower frantically screamed through the radio, "Pull up! Pull up! You're going to crash on the runway!"

In a panic, the pilot shouted back through the open microphone, "Which way is up? Which way is up?"

Those were the last words he was ever to speak. The plane crashed on the runway. Two days later he was buried. The follow-up report described the cause of the crash as *vertigo*—a medical term that means dizziness and swimminess of the head. It occurs when one has been revolved around and around until he experiences a loss of direction, balance, and sense of equilibrium. This was so in the case of this pilot. He lost his sense of direction. He lost his feeling of balance. He lost his equilibrium.

Isn't this what happens to us on many occasions? We look at our world, and everything is changing so fast and moving so rapidly that we lose our sense of direction. We are thrown off balance. We experience disequilibrium.

Sometimes we may feel extremely depressed, like the

young lady in her twenties who sat in my office. Her eyes
filled with tears. She stood up and paced the floor like a
caged animal. With agitation, she said, "I don't want to
live. Life is a big gyp. God could care less. The only person
who cares that I am alive is my mother, and the doctor says
that she has only three weeks to live."

For her, life was a downer. She was frantically crying
out, "Which way is up? Which way is up?"

In a sense, our whole society is caught in a state of violent vertigo. For instance, in the last ten years, violent
crimes have outstripped the population increase by 16 percent. Ten years ago there were 8,000 murders. Last year
there were 19,000, for an increase of something like 129
percent. Ten years ago there were 17,000 forcible rapes.
Last year there were 51,000, for an increase of about 200
percent. Ten years ago there were 172,000 aggravated as-
saults. Last year there were 412,000, for an increase of
about 139 percent. Last year alone we spent $1.5 billion on
vandalism, and $260 million just to repair vandalized
schools. To add insult to injury, since the Civil War we
have systematically sacrificed the lives of 565,000 American
soldiers through two World Wars, Korea, and Viet Nam.

We look at ourselves, observe our behavior, and know
that there is something frightening in what we see. We begin
to cry out, "Which way is up? What is right? What is
wrong? What is good? What is bad? What is truth? What is
error? Which trumpet sound is correct? How can I distin-
guish between the many uncertain noises and the tricky
drumbeats in the world?"

These are tough questions, and they have been around
for a long time. In fact, this is the warning of the Bible:
"Find the way up!" In biblical language, Christ told His
disciples that there would come a day of great calamity for
Israel, and, "When these things begin to take place, stand
up and lift up your heads, because your redemption is draw-
ing near" (Luke 21:28 NIV).

The point is that we live in a broken world marred by sin, disease, greed, and death. It is as though we exist under a sword of Damocles that hangs over our heads. We know that some day it is going to drop. The only problem is that we are not really sure just when it will happen.

Christ knew this and warned His disciples to become aware of the signs of the times. In Matthew 24 He spelled out vertigo in terms of false Christs, wars, famines, earthquakes, pestilences, persecutions, martyrdom, apostasy, and false prophets.

The apostle Paul knew this and warned Timothy that there would be a worldwide vertigo in terms of terrible times of great stress and unbearable trouble.

> People will be lovers of themselves, lovers of money, boastful, proud, abusive, disobedient to their parents, ungrateful, unholy, without love, unforgiving, slanderous, without self-control, brutal, not lovers of the good, treacherous, rash, conceited, lovers of pleasure rather than lovers of God—having a form of godliness but denying its power . . . .
>
> 2 Timothy 3:2–5 NIV

Quite a picture, isn't it? Almost sounds like a summary of the daily news. But then in Matthew 24:13 Christ shows us the way up and states, "But he who stands firm to the end will be saved" (NIV).

Which way is up? Christ says, ". . . stand up . . . lift up your heads . . . stand firm to the end . . . ." Sounds great! But *how?* How do we stand firm?

In answer, Christ lifts up four powerful words that can change the course of any situation—*be of good cheer!*

In the midst of crisis, "Be of good cheer!" In the midst of difficulties, problems, hardships, and devastating circumstances, "Be of good cheer!" Every time Christ mentioned those words, a miracle occurred. In the midst of the most excruciating crunch, He used the phrase "be of good cheer" and followed it with a miracle.

Experience a Miracle of Forgiveness

In Matthew 9 Christ had just delivered the Gadarene from his demonic possession. Christ had entered a boat and crossed the Sea of Galilee to His adopted hometown of Capernaum. There He found some men waiting for Him with a friend lying paralyzed on a cot. Christ perceived their faith and said to the paralytic, ". . . Son, be of good cheer; thy sins be forgiven thee" (Matthew 9:2 KJV). Christ performed a miracle of forgiveness.

Here was a man restricted to life on a cot. His whole world was circumscribed by that bed. He was in a state of vertigo. He had lost direction, balance, and equilibrium.

But why did Christ say, ". . . your sins are forgiven"? Such a statement brought the ire of the teachers of the Law down upon Him. In fact, they accused Him of blaspheming, but Jesus said, ". . . Why do you entertain evil thoughts in your hearts? Which is easier: to say, 'Your sins are forgiven,' or to say, 'Get up and walk'?" (Matthew 9:4, 5 NIV).

". . . Then he said to the paralytic, 'Get up, take your mat and go home' " (Matthew 9:6 NIV). The man did just that, and the crowd was astonished to the point where they praised God because He had given such authority to men. This man found the way up! It started with forgiveness.

"So what?" we ask. "What does this have to do with our situation?" In answer we would have to say, "Everything!" The fact is that the most important thing that can ever happen to anyone is to experience a miracle of forgiveness. The basis of this man's illness was inside himself, and in this incident there may be the first diagnosis of psychosomatic illness—a physical problem with a psychological cause. In all probability, Christ saw the bitterness, the cynicism, the resentment, and the hate. This must have been an angry man. All his friends were whole and well. All his friends enjoyed life, while he spent his time at their mercy in a state of dependency and hostility. It was a case of the soul and body working against each other. This man needed a miracle of forgiveness before his healing could ever take place.

Today doctors tell us that nearly 60 percent of all diseases they treat are psychologically and emotionally induced. This means that what goes on inside us has a great deal to do with how we function on the outside. When our lives get all tangled up, we become tense and tight. We lose our resistance and become vulnerable candidates for every traveling virus and germ invasion around.

Perhaps we can identify with a minister whom I met while speaking at a ministers' conference. Just before the start of the first session, he handed me a note which said, "My faith is still built on a rock." This triggered my memory, and I thought back to four or five years before, when we had counseled together because he was a pastor under pressure. He had ulcers and high blood pressure. About once a month he would break out in a terrible case of hives. The doctors told him he had an accelerated heartbeat because of tension and that he was a prime candidate for a heart attack.

Because of his constant illness, his church was upset, his wife was discouraged, and he was cynical and bitter. He was down and couldn't find the way up.

We talked at length through several sessions, and one day it hit me that this man needed the power of forgiveness and a renewed faith. We studied Matthew 16:18, 19 and literally internalized its words, ". . . on this rock I will build my church, and the gates of Hades will not overcome it. I will give you the keys of the kingdom of heaven; whatever you bind on earth will be bound in heaven, and whatever you loose on earth will be loosed in heaven" (NIV). Eventually he agreed to take every wrong, every hurt, every put-down, and every disappointment he had experienced in his ministry into the process of "binding and loosing.'' He even went so far as to work out a strategy in his prayer life where he put all of his pressures on the rock of faith in Christ. He literally lived by using the keys to the Kingdom. He experienced a miracle of forgiveness and renewed faith.

Later that same evening, after the session, he told me, ''My ulcers are gone. My blood pressure is down. My heartbeat is normal. I've learned to live with the keys of the Kingdom, and I have had the best health of my life over the past two years. For the first time in fifteen years of ministry, I can truthfully say I enjoy my work.''

''Be of good cheer; thy sins be forgiven thee.'' This is the way up!

Expect a Miracle of Faithfulness

Forgiveness is not all! There is a second step. It takes a miracle of faithfulness that is found in Matthew 14:27: ''. . . Be of good cheer; it is I; be not afraid'' (KJV).

Do you remember what was happening right then? Christ had just fed the five thousand. He told His disciples to go across the Sea of Galilee, dismissed the crowd, and went away to pray. When the disciples started the eight-mile row across the sea, they encountered a windstorm. The Bible says that during the fourth watch of the night, Jesus went out to them, walking on the sea. When the disciples saw Him walking on the water, they were terrified and thought He was a ghost. ''But straightway Jesus spake unto them, saying, Be of good cheer; it is I; be not afraid'' (Matthew 14:27 KJV).

Peter had a hard time really accepting the fact that it was the Lord. He wanted to test it out; so we hear him say, ''Lord, if it's you . . . tell me to come to you on the water'' (v. 28 NIV). Christ said, ''Come.'' Peter stepped out of the boat and started walking on the water to Jesus, but when he saw the wind, he panicked and started to sink. Peter suffered a case of vertigo and cried out, ''Lord, save me!'' ''Immediately Jesus reached out his hand and caught him.

'You of little faith,' he said, 'why did you doubt?' '' (v. 31 NIV). There, in the midst of a storm and a moment of faith turned to panic, Christ performed a miracle of faithfulness. He showed Peter the way up.

The fantastic part is that it will work for us. For instance, I remember one of the most dreaded days of my life. I had been called to visit a family that had just suffered bankruptcy. They had been millionaires, riding high in every respect. The recession hit, their financial house fell in, and in a matter of months they lost everything.

In January they were on top of the ladder of affluence, with a $250,000 home and all that goes with it. They had everything they wanted and more than they could use. Six months later they were paupers, with nowhere to turn and nothing to do. Everything was gone.

I arrived just after they had been stripped bare. I anticipated an atmosphere of gloom and despair. I walked to the door and rang the doorbell. A smiling woman greeted me, and my first thought was, "I must be at the wrong house." She said, "Come in, we have been looking for you. We are just getting ready to sing and to pray." Then I knew I was at the wrong house; so I asked, "Are you sure you are going to sing and pray?" "Yes," she answered. "Come on in. Isn't it wonderful! The Lord saved the piano. All the rest of the stuff is gone, but the piano is ours to keep. You're just in time to help us sing." Three children, the father, and I stood around the piano, holding hands. She sat down to play, and I thought that we would probably sing a funeral march or something like "Nobody Knows the Trouble I See." Do you know what we sang? The Doxology! Can you believe it? "Praise God, from whom all blessings flow; Praise Him, all creatures here below; Praise Him above, ye heav'nly host; Praise Father, Son and Holy Ghost. Amen."

They were moving from a $250,000 house to a two-bedroom apartment, with three children, and we sang the Doxology. They had lost everything but some clothes, a few odds and ends, a piano, and an old, beat-up station wagon, and we sang the Doxology. The question is how do we measure our worth? By thick carpets? Big drapes? Beautiful furniture? Stocks, bonds, and real estate? Or do we measure our lives by what it means to see the faithfulness of God as Christ comes walking to us in the midst of our failures and says, "Be of good cheer; it is I; be not afraid"?

This family has since regrouped. They are on the way back to better things, and they trust the faithfulness of God.

This is the way up! Just the time it looks as though we are going to sink. Just the moment we are ready to fall. That's when God performs a miracle of faithfulness and gives us the power to stand firm—*be of good cheer!*

Express a Miracle of Forcefulness

Forgiveness and faithfulness are two key concepts that come only from God, but there is yet another dimension. In John 16:33 Christ says to His disciples, "These things I have spoken unto you, that in me ye might have peace. In the world ye shall have tribulation: but be of good cheer; I have overcome the world" (KJV).

Not a very bright prospect, ". . . In the world ye shall have tribulation . . . ." Nonetheless, He was preparing them for a coming crunch when He would go away and they would be scattered abroad. It was difficult for His disciples to comprehend just what it all meant until after the miracle of His Resurrection and His words of John 20:21, 22, " '. . . Peace be with you! As the Father has sent me, I am sending you.' And with that he breathed on them and said, 'Receive the Holy Spirit' " (NIV).

Now the disciples had a new responsibility. They had to utilize the power of the Holy Spirit forcefully to continue the work of Christ in the world. They had received a miracle of forcefulness.

We have the same possibility. In fact, the Bible tells us

that we have the power to put down our enemies (*see* Psalms 44:5), to tread upon all the power of Satan (*see* Luke 10:19), to become more than conquerors (*see* Romans 8:37), and to overcome the world (*see* 1 John 5:4).

But the key to forceful power is found in the words of the apostle Paul:

For no one can lay any foundation other than the one already laid, which is Jesus Christ. If any man builds on this foundation using gold, silver, costly stones, wood, hay or straw, his work will be shown for what it is, because the Day will bring it to light. It will be revealed with fire, and the fire will test the quality of each man's work.

1 Corinthians 3:11–13 NIV

Here we have a choice. We decide the kind of material out of which to build our lives. If it's cheap wood, hay, and stubble, we will be destroyed. If it is precious gold, silver, and costly stones, we will overcome. We can play it any way we want to play it; say it any way we want to say it; and put it in any theological stance we choose, but all of us will be tested. There is no way to live in this world without going through the fire.

There is no gold without the refiner's fire. There is no steel without the heat of a blast furnace. There is no statue without the hammer and chisel. There is no diamond without the cutter's tool. There is no forceful life without the tribulation of the world.

This is the miracle of forcefulness—the power of the Holy Spirit that develops us into gold, silver, and costly stones.

Perhaps it is best illustrated in the life of Sadhu Singh—a Hindu who became a Christian. One day he was going up into the Himalayas to share his experience in a Buddhist monastery. Since the way was treacherous and obscure, he was being guided by a monk from the monastery. It was the beginning of winter, and suddenly a terrible blizzard came up from nowhere. The monk said to Sadhu, "We must hurry, or we'll freeze to death." As they were climbing a precipice, they heard a man calling for help from a deep chasm below. The monk tried to persuade Sadhu Singh to leave him behind and said, "God has brought him to this place, and he'll have to take care of himself. We must hurry or we, too, shall perish."

In reply, Sadhu Singh said, "No, God has brought me to this point to help my brother in need. You go on. I'll go to him." He lowered himself into the canyon and found the man suffering a broken leg from his fall into the chasm. Using his first-aid equipment, Sadhu fitted a splint to the man's leg, fashioned a stretcher out of his blanket, and helped the man to safety.

Then he literally tied the man to his back, and the two of them struggled together as they headed for the monastery.

Every step was laden with sweat, exertion, and pain, until the two were weary from exhaustion. After two or three hours of walking, they struggled over a rise and saw the lights of the monastery in the far distance. They speeded their steps but almost fell over an object lying across the path, covered in snow. Kneeling down, they brushed the snow away, only to find the monastery guide frozen to death in the blizzard.

In the process of exerting themselves, helping each other, and pushing themselves to near exhaustion, they had increased their circulation to the point where they had literally been spared from freezing and saved each other's lives.

Years later Sadhu Singh was asked to define the most important task in the world, and his reply was, "The most important task in the world is to learn how to carry a burden."

There is no way to be a Christian without a burden. Following Christ is not like rubbing Aladdin's lamp and having a private genie to appear and grant every whim. Following Christ is not a magic formula that plugs us into some psychic power to assume one-upmanship over those who have a different struggle. Following Christ is denying ourselves, taking up a cross, and becoming obedient, even if it means carrying a burden to death.

This is the way up! We stand firm to the end because we can experience a miracle of forgiveness, faith, and forcefulness. We can learn to "be of good cheer" and overcome the vertigo of the world.

9

You Can Live on Top
When the Bottom Drops Out

Perhaps the most perfect man who ever lived was a man named Job. When we read the biblical account of his life, by every criterion Job was an ideal person.

Job was a spiritual man. The Bible describes him as a person who was "perfect and upright. He feared God and turned away from evil" (*see* Job 1:1).

Job was a family man. He had seven sons and three daughters. Apparently they were very happy, because the Bible says they "feasted in their houses every day" (*see* Job 1:4).

Job was a successful man. The Bible says that his substance was seven thousand sheep, three thousand camels, five hundred yoke of oxen, five hundred donkeys, and a very great household. In fact he was looked upon as "the greatest of all men of the east" (*see* Job 1:3).

Job was a *holy* man. After his family had feasted, he sanctified them. Every morning he offered a burnt offering for each of his sons, in case they might have sinned (*see* Job 1:5).

Job was a religious man. The Bible says ". . . Thus did Job continually" (Job 1:5 KJV).

If Job were living in our day, he would be a man to be envied. We would say that Job had it made.

But suddenly the bottom dropped out. Everything that

had meaning, purpose, and made sense for him was lost. The Sabeans rustled all of his oxen and donkeys and killed all the herdsmen. Fire struck the sheep and the shepherds and burned them up. The Chaldeans raided the camels, carried them off, and put all the drivers to death. A whirlwind swept across from the desert, struck his eldest son's house, and killed all of Job's sons and daughters while they were dining (*see* Job 1:13–19).

To top it off, Job broke out in running sores from head to foot, and in disgust his wife said to him, "... Are you still unshaken in your integrity? Curse God and die!" (Job 2:9 NEB).

Then came his three best friends: Eliphaz, Bildad, and Zophar. Having heard of his great calamities, they came to console him. "For seven days and seven nights they sat beside him on the ground, and none of them said a word to him; for they saw that his suffering was very great" (Job 2:13 NEB).

Here he was: Job the affluent, Job the successful, Job the powerful: Everything was gone! Everything was wiped out!

At some time or other each one of us has probably been at the same place. The bottom has dropped out. Desperately we have tried to put the pieces back together and make the appropriate adjustments. We just don't know what to do. We rob Peter to pay Paul, and then rob Paul to pay Peter. It's like a vicious circle that never ends.

Sometimes we approach it like the young couple who had been married for about a year. They sat down one day to talk about their finances, and the wife said to the husband, "If we miss two payments on the refrigerator and one payment on the washing machine, we'll have enough money to make a down payment on a new television set."

Isn't this the way we try to handle it sometimes? We adjust here, adjust there, and try to adjust someplace else.

Then come the well-wishers and advisers. "Play it by ear. Do the best you can. Make the best of your circumstances," they say. One lady came into my office one day and said, "If I hear another person tell me to play it by ear or do the best I can, I'm going to scream. If you say it, I'm going to shoot you."

Obviously she was up to her ears in free advice about how to handle life when the bottom drops out. I didn't tell her to play it by ear, but I did think of a story that seemed to fit, and apparently it relieved some of the tension. Anyway, we laughed together.

Her statement reminded me of the man who bought a new Cadillac. His wife had never driven it. One day she took it to town for the first time. There was a parking space just barely big enough to accommodate such a big car; so, parking space being at a premium, she pulled up and backed in. She banged into the car behind her and banged into the car in front of her. After going through this same procedure two or three more times, she finally got the car settled in the tight space. With a sigh of relief, she got out of the car. A police officer was standing by, and in all innocence she said, "Tell me, Officer, how did I do?" He replied, "You did fine, lady, but tell me, do you always park by ear?"

Isn't this the way we often think? We beat and bang away, trying to solve our problems. We play it by ear and wish all of the time that we could find some plan or method that would work.

Well, what did Job do? Everything was gone. He was a sick man sitting in an ash pile. What did he do when the bottom dropped out?

Notice his action. "Then Job arose, and rent his mantle, and shaved his head, and fell down upon the ground, and worshipped" (Job 1:20 KJV). Rather strange, isn't it? Everything is lost and Job falls down on the ground and worships.

Notice his attitude. "In all this Job sinned not, nor charged God foolishly" (Job 1:22 KJV). Notice how he expresses this attitude. "For I know that my redeemer liveth, and that he shall stand at the latter day upon the earth: And though after my skin worms destroy this body, yet in my flesh shall I see God" (Job 19:25, 26 KJV).

What a fantastic outlook! Job learned to live on top when the bottom dropped out.

This is the same kind of testimony we hear from the apostle Paul. Look at all he had to undergo ". . . constant danger . . . . exhaustion, pain, long vigils, hunger and thirst, doing without meals, cold and lack of clothing" (2 Corinthians 11:26, 27 PHILLIPS). Look at all he had to suffer—that inexplicable thorn in the flesh. The Phillips translation calls it a "physical handicap—one of Satan's angels—to harass me and effectually stop any conceit" (2 Corinthians 12:7 PHILLIPS). How did Paul handle it? In his words, "Three times I begged the Lord for it to leave me, but His reply has been, 'My grace is enough for you: for where there is weakness, My power is shown the more completely' " (2 Corinthians 12:8, 9 PHILLIPS).

Paul found a resource in the grace of God to live on top when the bottom dropped out.

How do we get to that? It is one thing to talk about Job and Paul, and it is another thing to live on top right here in the twentieth century. So what is the formula? Where is the method?

Acknowledge Distress as a Fact

At the outset we have to acknowledge distress as a fact of life. Any way we look at it, we live in a broken world. Ever since Eden and original sin it has been a battle against the elements. Christ Himself said we would have to deal with tribulation (*see* John 16:33), and Paul made it clear to the Romans that:

. . . the creation was subjected to frustration . . . . the whole creation has been groaning as in the pains of childbirth right up to the present time. Not only so, but we ourselves, who have the firstfruits of the Spirit,

groan inwardly as we wait eagerly for our adoption as
sons, the redemption of our bodies.
Romans 8:20, 22, 23 NIV

As hard as we may try, there is no way to make heaven
on earth. We do have hope, however; for as we live this
life, we have the Spirit to help us in our weakness and make
intercession for us (*see* Romans 8:26, 27). In fact, Paul told
the Colossians:

As you live this new life, we pray that you will be
strengthened from God's boundless resources, so that
you will find yourselves able to pass through any experience and endure it with courage. You will even be
able to thank God in the midst of pain and distress
because you are privileged to share the lot of those who
are living in the Light.
Colossians 1:11, 12 PHILLIPS

In this regard, I met a man in Austin, Texas, and while
waiting for a banquet to start, asked him how things were
going. In answer, he said, "You might say that my family
and I are on the comeback trail." "The comeback trail?
That sounds interesting. What does it mean?" I asked. In
answer, he related that just two years prior he had been a
very wealthy man. The recession hit. He wasn't ready. He
lost everything he had. He turned to alcohol. His wife
turned to activities outside the home. His eldest son turned
to drugs, and in his words, "My whole family was tearing
apart."
Then he said, "One day my wife came to me and said she
couldn't stand it any longer. She wanted a divorce." This
was the last straw. He called a family conference and said,
"We've got to do something about this. We can't go on like
this anymore. What are we going to do?" To his surprise,
his twelve-year-old daughter stood up and said, "Daddy,
the first thing we have to remember is that God still loves
us."

Like a thunderbolt out of the sky, it hit them. "God still loves us." The family took inventory. They had lost everything tangible, but so what? It was wood, brick, chrome, and a little bit of this and a little bit of that.

Then he said, "We still had each other. We still had our health. We had opportunity, and we still had God." So he said, "We got on our knees and prayed for God's guidance. From that moment on we started on the comeback trail. I swallowed my pride and took a menial job. My wife went to work. The children are helping, and we have become a close-knit unit because we have really learned that God still loves us."

This is the way to handle distress, "God still loves us." The point is that God's love is not measured by circumstances. Job figured that out and never lost his integrity. Unfortunately, many people measure God's love by their level of affluence, their listing on Dun & Bradstreet, their profit-and-loss statement, or the number and value of their blue-chip stocks.

God is not capricious. God is not whimsical. God is not a respecter of persons. God is not a manipulator. God is not an exploiter, nor a sadist. His love is not measured by temporary fame, fortune, or affluence. God is building for eternity, and His love is measured on a hill called Calvary, where Jesus Christ died. Jesus said, "Greater love hath no man than this, that a man lay down his life for his friends" (John 15:13 KJV). Thus, God's love in us is illustrated in our attitudes and relationships, for "Hereby perceive we the love of God, because he laid down his life for us: and we ought to lay down our lives for the brethren" (1 John 3:16 KJV).

If we have achieved affluence, it obviously makes life more comfortable and is certainly no sin. However, it is no guarantee against the distress of life, and it is no sure symbol of a special dispensation from God.

In fact, Phillip Shoule and Jonathan Freedman did a study of over fifty-two thousand people who responded to a questionnaire on happiness. The results appeared in an article, "Your Pursuit of Happiness," in *Psychology Today*. The age range was from fifteen to ninety-five. The study involved people from all walks of life; they answered hundreds of questions about their areas of experience and about their beliefs concerning what might make people happy.

The consensus seemed to be that money can't buy happiness. Rather, happiness is an illusive mood of the mind, involving a delicate balance between what we think we ought to get out of life and what we really get. Further, happiness for most people in this study seemed to be the way in which circumstances were handled rather than the influence of the circumstances themselves.

Finally, the survey came up with four different attitudes that seem to be prerequisites to real happiness. First, there is the need for emotional security—disagreeing with the statement that good things can't last. Then there is the importance of the lack of cynicism—disagreeing with the more Machiavellian attitude toward human nature, or the idea of P. T. Barnum that "a sucker is born every minute." Next, there is the pursuit of a life-style which brings meaning or purpose—accepting values which have truth and are worth living by. Finally, there is the need for a sense of control— the feeling that we generate and control the good things in life, rather than just being pawns.

Obviously, it is easier to be happy if we are educated and have financial security, but all is in vain if we're overworked, battling too much stress, and experiencing a lousy homelife.

Obviously, it is easier to be happy if we are married to somebody we love, but if we never see each other and live as prisoners of loneliness, what difference does love make?

Happiness is a balance between expectations and achievements. It is taking the distresses of life in stride and using our circumstances for the glory of God. It is seeking first the Kingdom of God and His righteousness. It is knowing full well that all the things we need and can realistically handle will be given to us, as we live secure in the knowledge that God loves us.

This is the way to live on top—acknowledge distress as a fact of life, and remember that God's love is not measured by circumstances.

Activate Determination as a Force

Now back to Job: He had every right to be bitter, resentful, and hostile. To be sure, he had some tough moments, and we hear him cry out.

O that I might have my request, that God would grant what I hope for: that he would be pleased to crush me, to snatch me away with his hand and cut me off! For that would bring me relief . . . . What end have I to expect, that I should be patient? Is my strength the strength of stone, or is my flesh bronze? Or how shall I find help within myself? The power to aid myself is put out of my reach.

Job 6:8–13 NEB

In spite of it all, Job was a determined man. Not only did he worship God in the very height of his calamity, but he expressed a determined faith by saying, "Though he [God] slay me, yet will I trust in him . . . . He also shall be my salvation . . . ." There is a hook here, however, because Job's determination comes through even stronger as he states, ". . . but I will maintain mine own ways before him . . . . for an hypocrite shall not come before him" (Job 13:15, 16 KJV). On the one hand, "I will trust God regardless!" On the other hand, "I am going to be honest with myself and argue my cause, knowing that no godless man can appear before Him." This seems to be the reasoning of Job, and it illustrates the important truth that determination is the force of life. In our context, it is the power to live on top when the bottom drops out.

In all probability, each of us has been in the same double bind. We have had faith but made our beef known at the same time. The method is to trust God and put forth a determined effort in the same action.

Will it really work? It worked for Mary Jo. One day I got on an elevator in a hotel in Dallas, Texas, and came face-to-face with a woman in a wheelchair, who had a smile that looked like a beautiful sunrise. It literally radiated. Fascinated, I said, "My, you have a beautiful smile." In reply she said, "You're Dr. Walker, aren't you?" I answered in the affirmative and said, "How did you know me?" "I don't," she said, "in fact, I have never seen you before this convention, but I've listened to your tapes and worshiped with your congregation by tape for the past three years. In fact, it has been one of the sustaining forces in my life through some difficult times."

At this point, she had reached her floor, but I got off with her and talked with her in the hotel hall. Here is the story of Mary Jo as I wrote it down immediately after leaving her and returning to my room:

Three years ago I suffered an accident, and I was left paralyzed from the waist down. The first year was filled with resentment. The second year was a year of renewal. This year has been a year of rejoicing. Worshiping with your church has had a great part in helping me to see that I am a recipient of God's love. Really! I am the happiest I have ever been in my life.

The doctors told me I would probably never get out of bed or even sit up. But here I am, not only sitting up, but, look, I can even stand up! (At this point she stood up full length.)

Now the doctors tell me I will never walk, but if you come to this conference next year, plan to see me walking down this hall.

Determination is the force of life! It is the power to live on top when the bottom drops out.

Anticipate Deliverance as Fulfillment

Well the upshot was that Job hung in there until he got his case before God. To put it succinctly, deliverance is the fulfillment of faith. Job's faith in God paid off, and the Bible makes a profound statement, "So the Lord restored Job's fortunes and doubled all his possessions" (Job 42:10 NEB).

It's true, isn't it? We all like a happy ending, and some of us are still waiting and wondering, "When is it really going to happen to me?"

What do we mean by the fulfillment of faith, anyhow? How does this process actually work?

Technically, faith is the conviction of the truth of anything. It is a conviction, or belief, that looks to the future, to things that are not seen but hoped for, and it is the assurance that these things will be fulfilled as reality in the providence of God. (*See* Hebrews 11:1.)

Historically, faith is the story of mankind, our struggle with and our reaction to the forces of the environment and the limitations of human nature. Above all, it is the drama of mankind in relationship to a sovereign God; the plot shows how we live out that relationship in a broken world.

Practically, faith is committing our lives to the power of God, which we cannot see but have confidence in because of the revelation of God made known in Jesus Christ and experienced in our own personal encounters with the Bible as the Living Word.

Without faith we compromise freedom and have no plausible explanation for guilt, shame, responsibility, accountability, or the innate sense of "oughtness."

Without faith we cannot answer the question *Why?* Why do we feel sad when we hear music in a minor key? Why do we want to straighten an askew picture on a wall? Why do we shun the city dump, smile at the sight of a rose, and whisper in a funeral home?

Without faith we cannot explain the intimate experiences of human life—the instinct of a dog, the talent of an artist, the smile of a baby, and the warmth of a human touch.

Without faith we cannot provide standards. We can make a bomb, but we have no standards to control the use of that bomb. We can create biological warfare, but we have no standards to control its destructive use. Controls demand moral judgments and ethical values set against an absolute standard. Obviously, our track record in the world for making our values work is very poor, and the reason is that we have tried to live by sight rather than by faith.

Without faith we are silent in the presence of ultimate mysteries. It is very easy to become so scientific that we forget that the most important ingredient in a scientific experiment is the scientist himself: his hopes, dreams, fears, and failures. So often we shrug off the feelings of loneliness and isolation as mere by-products of conditioning, but it keeps gnawing away inside us that we need to relate to a Creator and fulfill the basic urge to love and be loved.

In psychiatrist Viktor Frankl's thought, the basic need in all of us is the will to meaning. Without meaning, life is walking death, and without faith as the guideline, meaning is a hollow shell.

Job was a man of faith, and it brought deliverance. When the bottom dropped out and Job had reached the end of himself, he put his whole trust in God and said:

> I know that thou canst do all things and that no purpose is beyond thee. But I have spoken of great things which I have not understood, things too wonderful for me to know. I knew of thee then only by report, but now I see thee with my own eyes. Therefore I melt away; I repent in dust and ashes.
>
> Job 42:2–6 NEB

Perhaps it is best explained by one of my parishioners, who is struggling for his very life with the dreaded disease of cancer. For many months he has wasted away with periodic improvements and subsequent declines. Finally, one day in his living room, we were talking about deliverance by faith, and he made this most significant statement: "I would like a miracle. I would like to live. If God heals me, I will be a living witness the rest of my life. However, if I die, I will go home to be with Him and enjoy the blessings of eternal life. The way I figure it, either way I can't possibly lose!"

This is deliverance as fulfillment, YOU CAN LIVE ON TOP WHEN THE BOTTOM DROPS OUT!

10

An Inside Look
at the Outside Life

Did you know that the type of defenses we use to cope with life may well determine the degree of success, happiness, or maturity we experience? Studies show that people with immature defenses are much more likely to see psychiatrists, suffer mental illnesses, and use drugs for emotional stability. Conversely, people with mature defenses have an enhanced ability to love, enjoy better health, are more satisfied with their vocations, and have stronger marriages. Because of this, it is important for us to take an inside look at the outside life. The question is how well do we cope? How efficient is our life-style?

When we read the Bible, it tells us that there is a deeper and more effective life-style available for every person. We read Psalm 1 and hear about a happy prosperous life, for

Happy is the man who does not take the wicked for his guide nor walk the road that sinners tread nor take his seat among the scornful; the law of the Lord is his delight, the law his meditation night and day. He is like a tree planted beside a watercourse, which yields its fruit in season and its leaf never withers: in all that he does he prospers.

Psalms 1:1–3 NEB

We hear this and say to ourselves, *It would be fantastic if I could have that kind of life-style—meditate on the Lord day and night, prosper in everything I do.*

We listen to the words of Jesus and find out about an imperturbable life—a life-style that can stand under every pressure because the foundation of faith is dug deep and established on a rock (*see* Luke 6:48).

We read Paul's letters and hear him constantly talk about a strengthened life from God's boundless resources, to the point where we will be ". . . able to pass through any experience and endure it with courage." In his words, "You will even be able to thank God in the midst of pain and distress because you are privileged to share the lot of those who are living in the Light" (Colossians 1:11, 12 PHILLIPS).

It all sounds super, but we take stock of ourselves and find out that it is a big order. We know we fall short. We continually make new resolutions. We renew our dedication to better living and sign up for all the new courses, but many times we wind up eating our own words.

It may be like the vacuum-cleaner salesman who knocked on the door of a beautiful home in a fashionable neighborhood. He was admitted to the living room by a very gracious housewife, and to her surprise he immediately opened up a box and ceremoniously dumped a sack of dirt, goo, and grime on her very expensive oriental carpet. In a confident voice, he said, "Lady, if this vacuum cleaner doesn't pick up all of this dirt and grime in two minutes, I'll eat every particle of it myself." With that she stood up and started for the kitchen. Startled, he asked, "Where are you going?" She replied, "I'm going to get a spoon. The power company called a little while ago, and the electricity is going to be off for the rest of the day."

In many ways, we experience the same kind of dilemma. We are threatened by change, frequent moving, and having to hurry everyplace we go. We are threatened by divorce, the problems of changing partners, and the fear of starting all over again. We are threatened by taxes being raised, financial deals falling through, and the loss of old friends. We eat our words, and we do it in terms of prolonged stress, ambivalent feelings, thwarted goals, and broken dreams. We become defensive, lose confidence, and develop ineffective coping mechanisms for handling our problems.

But this is the reason Paul wrote to the Colossians—to help them develop inside resources for a productive outside life. Paul wanted them to understand the full supremacy of Christ over all principalities and powers. Paul wanted them to experience the full redemption found in Christ and to learn to apply this redeemed life in practical, everyday living. In short, Paul tells us to take an inside look at our outside lives.

Well, it all sounds good, but how does it happen? Where is the formula?

In answer, Paul gives a three-point prayer for mature outside living:

> For this reason, since the day we heard about you, we have not stopped praying for you and asking God to fill you with the knowledge of his will through all spiritual wisdom and understanding. And we pray this in order that you may live a life worthy of the Lord and may please him in every way: bearing fruit in every good work, growing in the knowledge of God, being strengthened with all power according to his glorious might so that you may have great endurance and patience . . . .
>
> Colossians 1:9–11 NIV

Develop a Productive Purpose

Paul starts his prayer by asking God to do three things: (1) to fill us with the knowledge of God, (2) to help us live a life worthy of the Lord, and (3) to please Christ in every way.

At the outset, Paul seemed to know that there were three

basic needs in each of us—the need "to be," the need "to belong," and the need "to do." To make life count, we need to feel that we are of value and worth; we need to fit in and experience acceptance; we need to achieve success so that we have a sense of making a contribution and giving something back to the world.

Obviously this is no easy task! We called the sixties the age of anxiety, and now we brand the seventies as the *me* decade. In many respects, we have moved to a compulsive *I–me* syndrome and allowed the milk of human kindness toward others to curdle. As one psychiatrist states, "When I was growing up there was an egocentric greed for materialism. Now there is an egocentric greed for experience, and it's as though caring has been equated with losing."

What is the purpose of existence anyway? What is the beginning of a happy and productive life? To live for ourselves? To be wrapped in the *me* decade? In reality, the most bored, hectic, harassed, uptight, anxious, worried people in the world are those who are all caught up in themselves. They don't want the knowledge of God. They don't want to walk worthy of the Lord. They don't want to please Him. The thought of the day is, "If I can, I'll please me!" But this is contrary to every principle of the Bible. It is secularism at its highest. It is humanism at its worst. The purpose of living is found when we totally yield ourselves to the will of God, walk worthy of Him, and try to please Christ in every way.

What is the will of God? We have heard preachers and teachers tell us all our lives that we need to find the will of God. To put it succinctly, we have been ". . . predestined to be conformed to the likeness of his Son . . ." (Romans 8:29 NIV). But what does it mean to be like Christ? To paraphrase what Bishop J. C. Ryle says in *Holiness*, to be like Christ is to bear with and forgive others, even as Christ forgave us. It is to be unselfish, even as Christ pleased not

Himself. It is to walk in love, even as Christ loved us. It is to be lowly minded and humble, even as Christ made Himself of no reputation. It is to do the will of God, as it was the meat and drink of Christ to do His Father's will. It is to deny ourselves, to minister to others. It is to be meek and patient in the face of insults. It is to be full of love and compassion for sinners, to be bold and uncompromising with sin, and to do good in every situation.

This is the beginning of an inside look at our outside lives—to develop a productive purpose in a life-style that emulates Christ. This is living at its highest pinnacle.

Internalize a Productive Process

The second point of the apostle Paul's prayer tells us that we should bear fruit in every good work and grow in the knowledge of God. When we really analyze it, one of the most unique and interesting processes in all the world is the process of growth. By definition, growth is an increase in size, a differentiation in structure, and a change in form. But the wonderful thing about it is that it is unique and individual. No two things really grow alike. In fact, even in the case of identical twins there are differentiating characteristics and special features about each one.

Consider a special bamboo grass found in Ceylon. It grows sixteen inches per day and reaches a maximum of one hundred twenty feet in height, or the size of an eleven-story building. How would you like to mow that yard every Saturday?

Consider a seed smaller than the size of an acorn and less than an ounce in weight. Plant it, wait for about a thousand years, and it will become a full-grown giant redwood tree about three hundred sixty-five feet in height and some seventy-five feet at the base. It will contain enough lumber to build fifteen five-room houses.

Consider a tiny egg the size of the end of a little finger, but watch out when it reaches maturity, for it will be a blue whale that weighs over two tons and measures over twenty-five feet at birth. It will grow two hundred pounds per day and in seven months will weigh about twenty-three tons and measure some fifty-two feet in length. Within thirteen years it will reach full growth and measure eighty-five feet in length and weigh eighty to eighty-five tons—about the size of a modern submarine.

Fantastic, isn't it? All of this vividly illustrates growth as an increase in size, differentiation in structure, and alteration in form.

Isn't this our major problem in learning how to live? We stalemate and come down with a bad case of the "blahs" because we have never really internalized a productive process for living.

The Bible talks about the fact that we need to learn how to grow up. In Philippians 1:11 the Bible says we should increase in the fruits of righteousness. In Hebrews 6:1 the Bible says we should go on to perfection. In 1 Thessalonians 5:12, 13 the Bible says we should increase and abound in love toward one another and all people. In 1 Peter 2:2 the Bible says we should desire the sincere milk of the Word in order to grow. In 2 Peter 1:5 the Bible tells us we should make every effort to add to our ". . . faith goodness; and to goodness, knowledge; and to knowledge, self-control; and to self-control, perseverance; and to perseverance, godliness; and to godliness, brotherly kindness; and to brotherly kindness, love." For if we ". . . possess these qualities in increasing measure, they will keep [us] . . . from being ineffective and unproductive in [our] . . . knowledge of our Lord Jesus Christ." Finally, ". . . if anyone does not have them, he is nearsighted and blind, and has forgotten that he has been cleansed from his past sins" (2 Peter 1:5–9 NIV).

Obvious, isn't it? We are to increase in size, differentiate in structure, and alter in form. Perhaps it is best expressed by Paul in Ephesians 4:13:

"[That it might develop] until we all attain oneness in the faith and in the comprehension of the full and accurate knowledge of the Son of God; that [we might arrive] at really mature manhood—the completeness of personality which is nothing less than the standard height of Christ's own perfection—the measure of the stature of the fullness of the Christ, and the completeness found in Him.

AMPLIFIED

The thing the Bible is saying to us is that somehow in this Christian walk we ought to be internalizing a process that makes us mature. But how do we know a mature person? Should we carry signs around our necks that say, "I am a mature person. If you don't believe it, just ask me!" Or are there certain evidences in our outside lives?

Well, in answer let's try a coping test developed in a thirty-year study at Harvard and reported on by Ronald Kotulak in "Defending Yourself Successfully" in the *Miami Herald*. Our degree of happiness or unhappiness may well be the result of whether we face life immaturely, neurotically, or maturely. Let's take a hard inside look at our outside lives.

HOW WELL DO YOU COPE?

Immature

ACTING OUT: Do you have trouble handling your impulses? Do you drink to excess, walk away in the middle of a conversation, or have an extramarital affair because you "feel like it"?

FANTASY: Do you daydream about solutions to your problems? Do you have fantasies about running off with someone else after a fight with your spouse? Do you dream

	about being discovered as a star or important person?
PASSIVE AGGRESSION:	When you feel angry about something, do you hide it and get even in other ways? If your boss tells you to do something you don't want to do, do you tell him or her you'll do it, knowing that you don't intend to?
HYPOCHONDRIASIS:	Do you use illness as an excuse not to deal maturely with a problem?
PROJECTION:	Do you blame other people or things for your problems: "I would do better at work but somebody always has it in for me and blocks my promotions"?

Neurotic

REACTION FORMATION:	Have you had one bad experience that influences the way you deal with life in general? For instance, a person who has been hit by a car and later refuses to cross streets, go outside or see friends is overreacting.
INTELLECTUALIZATION:	Do you avoid the core of a problem by rationalizing? Do you blame troubles in your marriage, for example, on your spouse's coming from a "cold family"?
DISPLACEMENT:	When you are mad at your spouse, do you kick your dog or yell at the kids? If you are mad at your boss, do you come home and take it out on your spouse?

REPRESSION: Do you unconsciously internalize
                     strong feelings? Does your mind
                     block out disturbing feelings, like
                     the way you felt when your
                     mother died?

DISSOCIATION: Do you tend to take yourself out
                     of the picture during an emotional
                     crisis? In a severe tragedy, are
                     you unnaturally "cool"?

                     Mature

SUPPRESSION: Do you consciously make an ef-
                     fort not to let problems bother
                     you? When, for instance, you are
                     going to meet someone who al-
                     ways makes you mad, do you say,
                     "This time I'm not going to get
                     upset. I know I'm still going to
                     feel angry, but I won't show it"?

ALTRUISM: Do you share things with other
                     people and think of them in a be-
                     nign, nondemanding way?

SUBLIMATION: Do you substitute one set of so-
                     cially acceptable feelings for ones
                     that are unacceptable? Instead of
                     venting your feelings of aggres-
                     sion, for instance, do you go out
                     and jog or do some other socially
                     acceptable activity to release ten-
                     sions?

ANTICIPATION: Do you anticipate either joy or
                     pain at some future event? Do you
                     decide not to go to a party be-
                     cause a certain person will be
                     there who won't talk to you?

Well, how do you stack up? The point is that as we develop the productive process of bearing fruit and growing in the knowledge of the Lord, we continually mature into the image of Christ and are enabled to take part in more efficient outside living.

Exercise Productive Power

The third point of Paul's prayer is that we would be strengthened with all power according to His glorious might so that we might have great endurance and patience. In reality, Paul is using the Greek word, *dunamis,* for power, and obviously, it is the root word for "dynamite." Essentially this word, *dunamis,* has five shades of meaning: (1) *inherent power*—power residing in a thing by virtue of its nature; (2) *miracle power*—power to perform mighty works and deeds; (3) *moral power*—power of excellence and uprightness; (4) *influential power*—power to control through wealth, politics, and governments; and (5) *conquering power*—power to overcome with armies, forces, and hosts.

Thus, we would do no harm to the text to translate Paul's prayer in Colossians 1 in terms of *dynamite.* It would then read, "with all dynamite being dynamited according to the glorious dynamite." To bring it even closer home, we can say that Paul prayed for us to be dynamited with the nature of God, the miracles of God, the morality of God, the influence of God, and the conquering force of God. And the end result of all this power is not to demonstrate our own abilities or put on a one-man show. Rather it is to develop endurance and patience.

By *endurance* the Bible means "fortitude." It is the ability to bear pressure and turn distasteful problems into glorious victories. It is to endure in such a way that no situation can bring defeat. It is a sense of conquering stability.

By *patience* the Bible means "long-suffering." It is to

have a long spirit that is slow to anger and slow to retaliate. It is to have a quality of mind and heart which allows us to bear with people, to tolerate their unpleasantness, and to love them in spite of maliciousness and cruelty. It is to have a long fuse and a state of mind that is never driven to irritation or bitterness because of the folly and unloveliness of others.

This is the secret of the inside look at the outside life—to exercise the power of God to the point of endurance and patience, no matter what.

Perhaps the entire process can best be illustrated by the following letter of a man facing later-life decisions about career, future, life-style and God's will:

Dear Pastor,

This is to share a story of praise with you.

Seems like about five years ago, I was blessed with a word of knowledge while praying one evening on the way home from work. I was asking the Lord to show me how I could serve Him. He told me, "Be patient, I am pleased with your progress, and I have a plan for you, but you are not yet able to do it. Seek my word, by my Scripture and by my messengers, and heed my advice, and I will show you the way."

I think my "progress" for some time after that may have been less than pleasing to the Lord, because I don't recall any special verve or zeal on my part, nor any further explicit direction from Him. Even so, some time later when I was contemplating my future earthly prospects and opportunities in the remaining years of my working life—not praying, but just thinking—my thought process was:

1. I surely don't want to continue from 8:00 A.M to 5:00 P.M. every weekday at my present company 'til I am sixty-five.

2. I could retire at age fifty-five, but I really don't want to:
   a. run a Seven–Eleven store,
   b. or a Speedy Print shop,
   c. or be a management consultant,
   d. or anything I can think of.
3. So what *would* I do?

The answer came boldly into my mind: Become a lawyer! I don't remember now whether I recognized then or later that there was a qualifying adjective to be added to that imperative: Become a *Christian* lawyer!

The idea seemed almost preposterous. At my age . . . ? I had intended to go into law school at Notre Dame following my B.S. degree there in 1950, but I decided not to, because I had a wife and two children by then. In the years that followed, I had that aspiration from time to time, looked into night schools, and so forth. Finally, I concluded that I lacked the necessary drive and that it was just *too late*.

After all these years, could it be that God's plan was to use me as a counselor/lawyer—integrating Christian principles with legal services to my clients? It was amazing if true that He planned to use me in the very role that had been my suppressed desire for so long.

When I had done some investigating and contacted the law school of my choice in May 1974, I was told that the September '74 class was *full,* but that I might be accepted for enrollment in February '75. As I began to think more and more about the matter and to pray for guidance, things began to happen. I "accidentally" came across three new books dealing with the concept of Christianity and law in combination. Then one day I had an occasion to speak to Judge Kermit Bradford and asked for his candid advice on whether I was too old to

be starting out toward a career in law. His response
was so enthusiastic and so positive that I counted it as
part of the confirmation that I was on the right track.

Anyone who knows the Lord could finish this
story . . . . His blessings have exceeded that which
could be imagined.

—When I checked with the law school again, it
turned out there was room for me in the September '74 class after all.

—My situation at my company changed somewhat,
freeing me of some responsibility and pressure
. . . allowing me to handle the school load without
adverse effect on my job performance. (That
"change" was also a little heavenly sandpaper on
my pride and ego, and I thank the Lord for that
lesson.)

—I really enjoyed the classes, almost without excep-
tion, for nearly three years.

—I was graduated in June 1977 a Jurum Doctor Cum
Laude (with the glory entirely to God, especially
the "honors").

—After some intensive special study, I took the bar
exam in July . . . and learned two months later
that I'd *passed.*

—While a law student, I talked occasionally with a
good friend and a Christian lawyer in Marietta. We
had talked about working together someday, but I
knew he had taken an associate into his office and
had no room for me. At lunch, when I told Gene I
had passed the bar and would be sworn in the next
week, he told me his associate had just accepted a
post in Atlanta and was moving out . . . and he
invited *me* to move in. We *know* that the Lord will
lead us in every decision, business and personal.
And we know we will build up each other in faith
as well as support each other as lawyers.

I am *confident* that God's hand has been on my shoulder continuously in this endeavor, and that these past three years have been part of my "getting able" to do His plan for me. I am excited to see what will happen next! One day soon, He will tell me how I am doing . . . .

Pastor, will you pray with me that I will do the utmost from my side, and that I will be fully able—in mind, body, and spirit—when He calls me to do His will and His plan for me?

Praising His Holy Name,
BILL

It's true! Sometimes we get concerned about making our lives count. We have to step back and check out our lifestyles. Then, as was the case of Bill, we can see that Paul the apostle prayed a prayer that will help us take an inside look at our outside lives. We can have a productive purpose that will develop through a productive process into a productive power for successful living.

11

Positive Power
in Negative Times

The story is told of two mind readers who met on the street one day. One looked at the other and said, "You're fine. Can you tell me how I am?" In many ways, this is the way it is with our own lives. We look at other people and say, "They seem to be getting along so well, but what in the world is wrong with me?"

The truth is that we live in negative times. The biologists warn us that we are smothering our plants with overproliferation and overconsumption. The nuclear physicists tell us that there is the danger of radiation pollution. The biochemists tell us that overuse of drugs is creating a brain drain. The sociologists tell us that the "big rip-off" is becoming the American way of life. The psychiatrists tell us that this is the age of anxiety.

No wonder we ask ourselves, "Is there any future in futurism?" On one side of the coin there are those who paint a beautiful, Utopian future of optimism. They talk about the day when the population will decline, affluence will increase, and there will be an eternal energy source with plenty of food for everyone. On the other side of the coin there are those who sound a giant alarm of pessimism. They talk about a day of terrible global disasters, severe climatic changes, and massive crop failure. They portray a scene of drought, worldwide food shortages, and severe ecological upheavals.

Our problem is that we are caught in the crunch. Sometimes we get to the point where we just don't know where to go or what to do. We're frustrated! We're numb! We feel as if we have been pulled through a wringer!

As one seventeen-year-old said, "I'm not even sure I want to live in this world!" And what about all the statements we make about life in general? As a pastor and counselor I've kept a list. Here are some of the most prominent expressions of negative emotions that I have heard:

1. Sometimes I feel so fatigued I can't go another step.
2. Little things irritate me that never used to give me a problem.
3. I have lost my enthusiasm for things I really used to enjoy.
4. I get so careless about things that really used to matter.
5. What a drag it is just to get up in the morning.
6. I feel so insecure about so many things.
7. For the first time in my life I am worried about my job.
8. I don't have any friends. Everybody seems to be against me.
9. I always thought we had a good marriage, but now I wake up at night and wonder if my husband/wife is really faithful to me. I have no real reason to worry. I guess I am insecure.
10. I feel detached, disconnected, alone, and afraid. I just don't fit anywhere.
11. I get angry so easily and lash out at everything and everybody.
12. I lose my temper at the least little thing—I hyperventilate; I pout; I hold grudges; I am full of resentment and bitterness.
13. I feel as if I am holding up the whole world—my head

aches; my heart throbs; my nerves are always on edge.

14. I hate to say it, but I can't stand my children.
15. I am supposed to be a Christian, but I get bored reading my Bible. I fall asleep when I try to pray, and it is a drag to go to church on Sunday.

But then the Bible comes crashing through and gives us the message that we can have positive power in negative times.

The prophet Micah says we can be ". . . full of power by the spirit of the Lord . . ." (Micah 3:8 KJV). The prophet Zechariah says that it is ". . . Not by might, nor by power, but by my spirit, saith the Lord of hosts" (Zechariah 4:6 KJV). Christ says, "But ye shall receive power, after that the Holy Ghost is come upon you . . ." (Acts 1:8 KJV), and Acts 4:33 tells us, "And with great power gave the apostles witness of the resurrection of the Lord Jesus: and great grace was upon them all" (KJV).

"Incredible," we say. "How different! How powerful! How meaningful! How can that happen to us? How does such power take place in our lives?"

In answer Paul the apostle says there is a way out—a new life in Christ:

No condemnation now hangs over the head of those who are "in" Jesus Christ. For the new spiritual principle of life "in" Christ lifts me out of the old vicious circle of sin and death . . . . All who follow the leading of God's Spirit are God's own sons. Nor are you meant to relapse into the old slavish attitude of fear— you have been adopted into the very family circle of God and you can say with a full heart, "Father, my Father." The Spirit Himself endorses our inward conviction that we really are the children of God. Think what that means. If we are His children, we share His treasures, and all that Christ claims as His will belong to all of us as well! Yes, if we share in His sufferings we shall certainly share in His glory.

Romans 8:1, 14–17 PHILLIPS

Here in five verses of Scripture is the model for achieving positive power in negative times. In contemporary terms, it is a four-phase process: (1) *Change your walk:* ". . . the new spiritual principle of life 'in' Christ lifts me out of the old vicious circle of sin and death . . . ." (2) *Follow the Spirit:* "All who follow the leading of God's Spirit are God's own sons." (3) *Renounce fear:* "Nor are you meant to relapse into the old slavish attitude of fear—you have been adopted into the very family circle of God . . . ." (4) *Claim your heritage:* "If we are His children we share His treasures, and all that Christ claims as His will belong to all of us as well!"

Now, just what does all this mean?

Change Your Walk

To begin with, it means that we have to experience a change in life purpose. This comes about through repentance on our parts, whereby we turn away from sin and turn to God. In reality, it is much more than being sorry for our misdeeds; it involves the actualization of the gift of faith in our lives. It is being lifted out of the ". . . old vicious circle of sin and death" (Romans 8:1 PHILLIPS).

Sin? What is sin? In the words of Karl Menninger, "Whatever became of sin?" In many respects, it has become a rather respectable word, veiled in terms of immorality, ethics, and antisocial behavior. However, Menninger tells it like it is when he writes, "I believe there is 'sin' which is expressed in ways which cannot be subsumed under verbal artifacts such as 'crime,' 'disease,' 'delinquency,' 'deviancy.' "

But when the Bible talks about sin, what does it mean? In

the Old Testament, sin is the changed status of an acting agent, as illustrated in the life of King Saul. He degenerated from the first king of Israel, head and shoulders above every man in Israel, to a self-condemned fugitive seeking deathbed wisdom from a witch in En-dor. In the Old Testament, sin is the quality of a premeditated act, as illustrated in the life of King David. He willfully plotted the death of Uriah to legitimize his affair with Bathsheba. In the Old Testament, sin is rebellion as expressed in the golden calf created by the Israelites while Moses was on the mount receiving the Commandments of the Lord.

In the New Testament, sin is missing the mark when we have the ability to hit the bull's-eye. It is stumbling and falling down when we have the capacity to walk straight. It is an inherent meanness and badness classified as ". . . the powers of this dark world and . . . the spiritual forces of evil in the heavenly realms" (Ephesians 6:12 NIV). It is transgression of God's law, for "Everyone who sins breaks the law; in fact, sin is lawlessness" (1 John 3:4 NIV). It is neglect of opportunity, for James says, "Anyone, then, who knows the good he ought to do and doesn't do it, sins" (James 4:17 NIV).

Sin is the underlying negative force that cripples our growth and bogs us down under the pile of guilt, condemnation, and degeneration. But Paul tells us, " . . . live not after the dictates of the flesh, but after the dictates of the Spirit" (Romans 8:1 AMPLIFIED). And isn't this where the rub comes? Isn't this what Christianity is all about—trying to hammer out a life that rises above the lower and baser elements of life?

But what does it mean when we talk about the flesh? Actually, it is a very interesting word which originally meant that which can be stripped away—that which can be drawn out—that which can be peeled off. It is the veneer—the false covering. It is human nature that is devoid of divine influence. It is the part of us that is prone to sin. It is the impetus for low living and baseness that disregards God's power and Spirit.

Galatians 5:19–21 puts it on the line:

The acts of the sinful nature are obvious: sexual immorality, impurity and debauchery; idolatry and witchcraft; hatred, discord, jealousy, fits of rage, selfish ambition, dissensions, factions and envy; drunkenness, orgies, and the like. I warn you, as I did before, that those who live like this will not inherit the kingdom of God.

NIV

The basic question is, "Do I live my life by the dictates of the flesh? Do I live my life by the baser emotions that I can't control? Do I make my decisions based on my carnal desires?" When we live by the flesh, we become depressed. When we live by the flesh, we become hostile. When we live by the flesh, we become anxious and worried. When we live by the flesh we are easily bored and fatigued.

Follow the Spirit

But there is a better way! When we live by the Spirit, we mount up with wings as eagles. We run and are not weary. We walk and don't faint (*see* Isaiah 40:31). When we live by the Spirit, we are sealed—marked out—inscribed and branded with Christ (*see* Ephesians 1:13). When we live by the Spirit, we have access to the Father, without fear or reservation (*see* Ephesians 2:18). When we live by the Spirit, we are strengthened and reinforced in the inner life (*see* Ephesians 3:16). When we live by the Spirit, we sing psalms, hymns, and spiritual songs. We make music in our hearts to the Lord. We learn to be thankful to God at all times for everything, and we fit in with one another because of our common reverence for Christ (*see* Ephesians 5:18–21).

The difficulty is that we are a lot like Jacob: always playing games—always deceiving, always trying to get away with the "con" game when we know it will catch up with us. Jacob stayed in a bind. He struggled against his twin brother before he was born; he had to run away from home when he was young because he deceived his brother and his father in collusion with his mother. He worked fourteen years to earn the wife he wanted, only to have his beloved Rachel die a premature death. Later, his favorite son, Joseph, was sold into bondage. Benjamin, his youngest, was detained in Egypt. What a tragedy!

But what a change! Jacob finally got it together. He was transformed. He became transparent. How powerful his witness when he explained the heritage he was leaving to posterity. We say that we worship the God of Abraham, Isaac, and Jacob, but it took Jacob a long time to learn to live by the dictates of the Spirit. He didn't really change until he met God face-to-face at Peniel. Through the Spirit of God, Jacob and Esau were reconciled. Jacob learned to live in the Spirit.

The whole thing is that we don't like to be broken. The Spirit of God is not like lightning. It is like electricity. It has to have wires. It has to have a bulb. It has to have a vessel in which to be tabernacled. We are the alabaster box, and when we are broken, the Spirit of God is released.

In our brokenness there is power, and we are enabled to ". . . follow the leading of God's Spirit . . ." (Romans 8:14 PHILLIPS) to the point where Galatians 5:22, 25 will truly come alive: "But the fruit of the Spirit is love, joy, peace, patience, kindness, goodness, faithfulness, gentleness and self-control . . . . Since we live by the Spirit, let us keep in step with the Spirit . . ." (NIV).

Perhaps this process is best illustrated by a long-distance telephone call I received from a man in New York who had just listened to one of our radio broadcasts. For over an hour he poured out bitterness, resentment, and hate against an ex-wife from whom he had been divorced for ten years. In a rage, he shouted over the telephone, "She had the nerve to call me and tell me that my two sons are in deep trouble. Now that the children are teenagers and she can't handle them she wants my help. She was unfaithful! She left me! She took my children! I hate her! I'm trying to be a Christian, but I hate her! Yet it's true, my children need my help. What shall I do?"

In reply, I asked him, "What would the Spirit have you do?" He thought about that for a while and said, "Well, I ought to get things straightened out. We should work together on these problems, but it is so hard. She did me so dirty." I continued to encourage him to seek God's guidance and help—to let the Holy Spirit really work through him toward both his ex-wife and his children. We prayed together and hung up.

About a week later, he called back. His first words were, "A miracle has taken place. I can't say that I love her, but I don't hate her. I can't say that I really approve of all that she is doing, but we are talking together. We've made an agreement. We are going to try to work together to help our two sons through their problems. She is still going her way, and I'm going mine, but at least we're going to cooperate on this."

This is it! Change your walk! Follow the Spirit! It pays rich dividends!

Renounce Fear

Then Paul moves into phase three: "Nor are you meant to relapse into the old slavish attitude of fear—you have been adopted into the very family circle of God and you can say with a full heart, 'Father, my Father' " (Romans 8:15 PHILLIPS).

Perhaps the most crippling emotion in our lives is that blind, apprehensive fear called anxiety. Anxiety speaks to us from crowded city sidewalks, jammed-up freeways, sky scraping buildings, and quick lunches from vending machines. Anxiety blares at us from the headlines, whines at us from the stage, laughs at us from the advertisements, and clatters at us from Wall Street. Anxiety writes the black statistics of war, rape, murder, and divorce. Anxiety tortures us with too many mortgages, too many martinis, and too many drugs, and at the base of anxiety is fear.

It was fear that kept Jonah from going to Nineveh to preach. He was afraid they wouldn't hear his words. It was fear that made Samson betray his secret to Delilah. He didn't want to lose her favors, and he was afraid of losing status in her eyes. Because of fear, David plotted for Uriah's death. He had to cover up his tracks. He was afraid of God, afraid of Nathan, afraid of the people, afraid for his position.

Because of fear, a businessman said to me, "Things are so bad I can't even get out of bed in the mornings. My business is still going. In fact, it's operating in the black, but I'm so worried; I'm so afraid that I lie in bed in the fetal position and shake like a leaf until noon every day." Because of fear, a thirteen-year-old girl will not go into her own house in mid-afternoon. She stays with a neighbor until her parents return from work in the evening. She lives paralyzed by fear.

The crucial point is that society programs us to fear. Actually, it has been estimated that every American individual receives over five hundred advertising messages every day. We only internalize about seventy-five of these, but what do they suggest? It has been further estimated that the average American adult watches television about six and a half hours per day. The point is that our senses are being bombarded by a pagan world system, and it says, in essence, "If we can't get you consciously, we'll get you subliminally." In fact, studies show that through a combination of subliminal stimuli and posthypnotic suggestion the anchor points of values, morals, concepts, and convictions can be shifted until our discriminating ability is impaired. This is why Romans 12:2 tells us, "Don't let the world around you squeeze you into its own mould, but let God re-mould your minds from within . . ." (PHILLIPS).

This is positive power for negative times, "For God has not given us a spirit of fear, but a spirit of power and love and a sound mind" (2 Timothy 1:7 PHILLIPS). And this power comes from Christ. He has power to save (*see* Isaiah 63:1); He has power to forgive sins (*see* Matthew 9:6). He has all power in heaven and earth (*see* Matthew 28:18). He has power over nature (*see* Luke 8:25). Christ is the power that drives out fear. What we are in Him determines what we are in the world. If we have no power in the world to meet the negative forces of the world, it is because we have no power in Him.

Claim Your Heritage

This brings up the final phase, "If we are His children we share His treasures, and all that Christ claims as His will belong to all of us as well!" (Romans 8:16, 17 PHILLIPS).

The point here is that what God was in Christ, Christ is in us. What God did in Christ, Christ is doing in us. The relationship that God the Father has with the Son, is the relationship that Christ, as the Son, has with us. What we have in Christ, we have in God. Through Christ we are infused with the power of God. Through Christ we are identified with the power of God. Through Christ we are imputed with the power of God. What God did at Calvary through His Son, He has done in us. In Christ we can live, move, and have our being. In Christ we are overcomers over death, hell, and the grave. In Christ there is power to defeat every foe.

Our heritage is the power of authority. Christ says, "I tell you the truth, anyone who has faith in me will do what I have been doing. He will do even greater things than these, because I am going to the Father" (John 14:12 NIV).

Will this really work? Obviously, the last word belongs to God, and there is no way we can usurp His sovereignty. We always see through the glass darkly. Yet, in the miracle, He gives us insight and glimpses into His power and authority over all the world. When we believe, God listens. When we exercise faith, God moves mountains.

As an example, notice my father's testimony of a miracle that confirmed the faith of my grandparents and fulfilled their prayers for my father:

> I was born with a severe heart condition, commonly known as a blue baby, and the family doctor said that I would not live. Mother and Father worried and prayed for my survival, but I rather grew worse. Father told me later that he kept me in his arms most of the time to keep up my blood circulation.
>
> Finally, however, when hope seemed to have vanished, Mother and Dad placed me on the bed, and kneeling there, they cried out to God for my healing. At the same time they dedicated me to whatever service the Lord wished for me to perform. Their prayers were answered. I was completely healed; and from that day to this (I am 69 years old at the time of this writing), I have never had a pain in my heart, neither has it ever given me any trouble. The Lord has had His hand on my life. It is He who said, "I am the Lord that healeth thee" (Exodus 15:26).

Our heritage is the power of affection. Christ says, "As the Father has loved me, so have I loved you. Now remain in my love" (John 15:9 NIV). The apostle Paul gets in the act and says, ". . . God has poured out his love into our hearts by the Holy Spirit, whom he has given us" (Romans 5:5 NIV). To *pour out* is to give in great abundance and in large amounts. It means to "inundate" or "flood." We do no harm to the rendering to say that the Love of God floods our inner selves by the Holy Spirit.

However, it is one thing to know about this heritage and quite another to really exercise it. Somewhere I read about an American family that met a French family visiting here in America. Several years later the American family returned the visit in France, but by this time both families had small boys about the same age. Since neither family was bilingual, there was concern about how the boys would get along during the visit. To everyone's surprise, they got along very well. When the visit was over and the American family was headed home, the parents asked their son, "How did you manage to get along so well when you couldn't communicate?" The little boy replied, "Oh, it was nothing. He speaks French, but he laughs in English."

Language is more than words. It is the meeting of spirits. It is Christ saying, ". . . Now remain in my love" (John 15:9 NIV).

Our heritage is the power of acceptance. Christ prayed to the Father:

> I in them and you in me. May they be brought to complete unity to let the world know that you sent me and have loved them even as you have loved me. Father, I want those you have given me to be with me where I am, and to see my glory, the glory you have given me because you loved me before the creation of the world.
>
> John 17:23, 24 NIV

The beauty here is that God accepted us in Christ from the very beginning. The catch is that we have to accept Him as Lord of our lives in order to be accepted by God. To be accepted is to receive a new spirit (*see* Ezekiel 11:19). To be accepted is to receive a new heart (*see* Psalms 51:10). To be accepted is to receive a new mind (*see* Romans 12:2). To be accepted is to receive a new inner power (*see* 2 Corinthians 4:16). To be accepted is to be regenerated (*see* Titus 3:5).

To be accepted is to receive a new song (*see* Revelation 15:3). To be accepted is to receive a new name (*see* Revelation 3:12).

Perhaps it is best illustrated by the story of a grammar-school teacher during the early days of school integration. In her school there was only one black boy, and for the first few days he was left alone by students and faculty alike. It worried this teacher, and she resolved to try to do something to help this boy be accepted. After all, he didn't ask to be born, but he was born. He didn't ask to be sent anywhere, but he was sent. All he needed was a chance.

Finally, one day at recess she saw him standing all alone by the fence. Suddenly a drama unfolded before her eyes. Some of the white kids walked over to where he was standing. One of them pulled a piece of bubble gum out of his pocket and handed it to the black boy. He didn't want to take it at first, but decided to accept. He unwrapped it, started to put it in his mouth, hesitated, and then broke it in half and gave half of it back. Everybody just stood there kind of awkwardly looking at each other when someone threw the black kid a ball. He caught it and threw it back. It came back to him, and he threw it again. Soon they were throwing the ball all around, and the next thing she knew, they were playing together. There was a mutual power of acceptance—a heritage that comes with the package of the human race.

You see, the problem is not at the grass roots. There are no politics there. There are no power structures there. There are no exploiters and manipulators—no axes to grind. It is a matter of sharing bubble gum, throwing a ball, and learning to play together. It is practicing the power of acceptance. God did it for us long ago. We were all aliens and foreigners. For Christ's sake He made us children and heirs.

There is no doubt about it! You can have positive power in negative times. Here is what it will take: (1) Change your walk. (2) Follow the Spirit. (3) Renounce fear. (4) Claim your heritage.